PLANTING REPRODUCING CHURCHES

PLANTING REPRODUCING CHURCHES

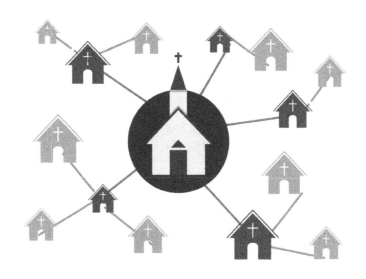

ELMER L. TOWNS

DESTINY IMAGE® PUBLISHERS, INC.
P.O. Box 310, Shippensburg, PA 17257-0310
"Promoting Inspired Lives."

This book and all other Destiny Image and Destiny Image Fiction books are available at Christian bookstores and distributors worldwide.

Cover design by Eileen Rockwell
Interior design by Terry Clifton

For more information on foreign distributors, call 717-532-3040.

Or reach us on the Internet: www.destinyimage.com.

ISBN 13 TP: 978-0-7684-1762-3
ISBN 13 EBook: 978-0-7684-1763-0
ISBN 13 LP: 978-0-7684-1764-7
ISBN 13 HC: 978-0-7684-1765-4

For Worldwide Distribution, Printed in the U.S.A.
1 2 3 4 5 6 / 21 20 19 18

CONTENTS

FOREWORD

Why do new churches represent the biggest movement of God today? Why do some church plants fail and others succeed? What's the difference between starting a church and starting a *reproducing* church?

If anyone in North America has the leadership chops and expertise to address these questions, it's Elmer Towns. His life experience is almost without parallel. When blended with his incredible teaching and storytelling abilities, the result is a lifetime of wisdom and biblical insight that can save you many scars and inspire you to a bigger dream.

Our friend, colleague, and mentor, Elmer Towns, has been researching and analyzing long enough to see through fads and discern what's truly going to make a difference. Some 50 years ago, he wrote *The Ten Largest Sunday Schools and What Makes Them Grow,* predicting the coming explosion of the megachurch movement in North America. That book was also among the first to explain the principles and best practices of the rising Church Growth Movement.

His newest book, *Planting Reproducing Churches,* could be just as revealing. He researched scholarly books on the explosion of

Christianity in the Global South (Africa, South America, Indonesia, and India) and the Oriental Crescent (China and South Korea). This included traveling to these areas to see firsthand what was happening. He visited 20 nations in the past 4 years, preached in some of the largest churches in the world, and had long chats with their leaders. He tried to look at their expressions of Christianity through their "indigenous eyes."

His insight will enlighten you, but you'll also be infected by his contagious love for the church and the way he pushes us toward growth by multiplication rather than only by addition. Just as God told the first couple, *"Be fruitful and multiply...,"* so Jesus told the disciples to *"go...to everyone...the entire world...baptizing them...disciplining them...until you reach every ethnic group"* (Gen. 1:28; Matt. 28:19-20 ELT). Isn't that also multiplication? You will love the way Towns describes the church as a growing body and gives us a new feeling about growing churches around the world.

Towns says church planting not only works as an evangelistic method, but it's on the increase, expanding on what we documented in our book *Viral Churches: Helping Church Planters Become Movement Makers.*

In fact, Towns goes so far as to say that the effectiveness of the evangelistic crusade is diminishing and the newest evangelistic method that God seems to be anointing is the return to the first and most effective method of all: church planting. That's why he believes that if each church would plant other churches, we could hasten the day when Jesus Christ will return (see Matt. 24:14).

Church planters will thrive on this book, but it's not for them alone. Some 80 percent of the churches in America have plateaued or are declining. The leaders in these churches should read this book because of the following:

- They can get motivated to plant a satellite church as a multisite church.

- They can learn innovative steps and methods to begin another church (six different methods to plant a church are included).

- They can sharpen their counsel for foreign missions supported by their church.

- They can open up their church to social media outreach and church planting.

- They can get vision on how to expand a plateaued church and give it new energy.

- They can break their barriers of limited seating, limited geography, and ethnic or economical boundaries. Wouldn't it be great to have a "limitless" church?

Towns has been a mentor to me (Ed) for decades—from when I was his student, to then being his coauthor, and now as a colleague. His love for the church has always been contagious, and you will see that love in the pages of this book.

I (Warren) love the way that Towns uses specific churches from today to illustrate his insights from Scripture. I also love how incredibly practical he is. To me, his final chapter, "46 Practical Steps to Plant a Church," full of wisdom, examples, and great stories, in itself is worth the price of the book.

We both agree that church planting is near to the heart of God, so if you want to touch God, get close to church planting. And when you do, God will get close to you and touch you as well.

Sincerely yours,

Ed Stetzer (@edstetzer) and Warren Bird (@warrenbird)

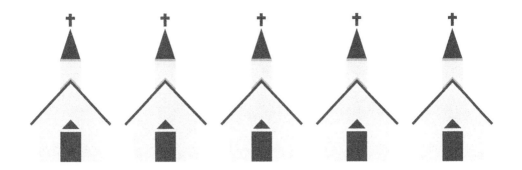

Part One

THE FOUNDATION OF REPRODUCING CHURCHES

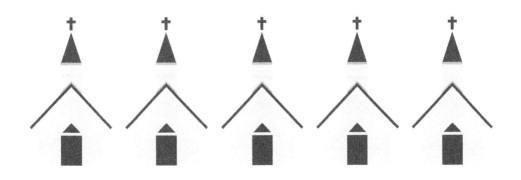

CHAPTER 1

VISION AND PASSION FOR CHURCH PLANTING

Are you interested in planting a church? If so, you will create something that is alive, vital, and majestic. There is a parallel between planting a church and planting a seed in the ground. Planting places a kernel of corn in the earth that came from a living ear of corn. A kernel has life within itself, and that seed will produce a living stalk of corn that has three or four ears of corn. And each ear will produce approximately 708 kernels of corn. Each kernel will contain the life of the original kernel. When a stalk of corn is growing, the original kernel will multiply into 3,000 stalks of corn, and when all are reproduced year after year, within four years they will produce 32 million kernels of corn just like the original one.

Multiplication is the strategy by which God created the world. Every living organism in the world can reproduce a multitude of itself from one seed. That's God's strategy in planting churches. One church can reproduce itself into a large denomination. Reproducing churches can complete the Great Commission in our lifetime.

A church planter and/or team with eternal life in them will plant a new church that has life to reproduce itself. From a kernel comes an ear of corn. From a born-again church planter comes a living church, that is, an assembly of other believers. And the life energy of each believer can reproduce another believer, or another church. One kernel of corn can produce a whole field of corn. One church can lead to reproducing churches. God calls this multiplication.

God created vegetation with a seed that could reproduce another plant like itself. That also is called "multiplication."

Then God began to create animal life with life-giving seed within each animal—male and female—producing another just like themselves. The same pattern was followed with crawling insects, flying birds, and fish swimming in the sea. Each had the seed of life within itself to produce another like itself.

Then God created man and woman, God blessed them and said, *"Be fruitful and multiply. Fill the earth and govern it. Reign over the fish in the sea, the birds in the sky, and all the animals that scurry along the ground"* (Gen. 1:28 NLT). Did you see the command? Multiply. What God commanded the first pair of humans is included in the Great Commission today.

A church is Jesus, and when you plant a church, you are planting the life of Jesus that will become His life in all the believers in that assembly. Yes…the church is Jesus![1] Isn't the church called "the Body of Christ" (see Eph. 1:22-23)? So when you describe the characteristics of a local church, you're describing the nature of Jesus Himself.

Saul, the religious Pharisee, was blinded to the light of Jesus Christ, whom he hated. Saul went through every house in Jerusalem arresting Christians (see Acts 8:3); then he got authority to go to Damascus to arrest more Christians and bring them back to

Jerusalem. As Saul approached Damascus, Jesus appeared to him in a blinding light. Because he was spiritually blind, Christ blinded him physically. He cried out, *"Who are You, Lord?"* (Acts 9:5).

"I am Jesus, whom you are persecuting." (Acts 9:5). Did you see that shift in the direct object? When Saul was persecuting Christians, he actually was persecuting Jesus. Jesus is the church because He lives in each believer who makes up the church, and then He promised that *"for where two or three are gathered together in My name, I am there in the midst of them"* (Matt. 18:20). So when Saul persecuted Christians, he was persecuting Jesus.

When you plant a church, you are planting Jesus. You are placing Him in a community so He can, through every member, invite outsiders to *"follow Me..."* (Mark 1:17).

So when you think about church planting, do not begin your strategy with organizational techniques, and don't think first of a doctrinal statement or even a chartering statement. And beyond that, a church is not about a denomination, and surely it is not the building. Think of a new church as a new organism; it is planting Jesus Christ in the community.

THE FIRST MENTION OF CHURCH IN SCRIPTURES

A new church is a majestic thing. Look at the first time the word *church* occurs in Scripture spoken by Jesus: *"...I will build My church..."* (Matt. 16:18). Jesus was pointing His disciples to a new entity that He instituted. There was no church in the Old Testament; God had worked through the Jewish nation as His primary plan. There was a king to lead them and prophets to deliver His word to them. There was a temple in Jerusalem and a priesthood to lead the Jewish nation in worship. But there was nothing as unique as a church.

When Jesus said, *"I will build My church,"* He was looking beyond the cross to a group or assembly of His followers who would carry His message to the entire world (Matt. 16:18). There are five things about the church that can be seen in the five words of this statement:

1. *"I...."* Jesus is the church builder, and He is the *church planter.* Technically, a church may be planted by a person, couple, or team of people who plant a new church, but Jesus is doing it through them. Because He loves all people and wants all people to believe in the message of the cross, and because it is His purpose to win all nations and rule over them, Jesus begins each new church.

2. *"I will...."* That word *will* is future tense. Jesus looks to the future and sees that His church is the vehicle through which the message of salvation will be preached to the world. The church is not a continuation of the Old Testament but is built on its foundation. It will become the vehicle through which Christ will ultimately deliver the message of salvation to lost people.

3. *"I will build...."* The word *build* suggests a continuous action, predicting that Jesus would continually be building His church. What Jesus began in the Book of Acts He continued throughout the Roman Empire. When the massive Roman Empire collapsed, one smaller empire or nation came into existence after another, and through all of those nations the church continued. Why? Because the church was a divine Person; it was Jesus Christ being preached to the unsaved. The church crossed geographical barriers,

cultural barriers, ethnic barriers—all to penetrate the lives of people who believe in Him. Together they became the majestic Body of Christ, represented by local churches all over the world.

4. *"I will build My...."* Do you see that possessive pronoun? The church belongs to Jesus Christ. Many individuals or groups have claimed possession of the church. Some call it Presbyterian, some call it Methodist, or Episcopal, or Pentecostal. In some places, it does not even have a name; it is just Jesus' people assembled together. Some have referred to it as "my church." But it doesn't belong to one person. It does not belong to the official board, the pastor, or the people. The church belongs to Jesus Christ.

5. *"I will build My church...."* The word *church* is the Latin word *ecclesia*, which means "an assembly or gathering of people." The church is a group of people. In the original language, it is made up of a preposition, *ek*, meaning "out," and a verb, *kalew*, which means "to call." Jesus calls His people out from the world. He calls people from themselves, from sin, or anything that would take His place.

But there is a second part to Jesus' call: He calls people to Himself. When you join a church, you don't just come into a denominational church; rather, you come to Jesus, for He is the church. You are called to know Him and make Him known.

Every Christian is like a kernel of corn, and the church is an assembly of many kernels on an ear of corn. Corn can be eaten for nourishment, or corn can be planted for multiplication.

Life in that kernel of corn starts with death. Jesus explained the death formula for the reproduction of life: *"I tell you the truth, unless a kernel of wheat is planted in the soil and dies, it remains alone. But its death will produce many new kernels—a plentiful harvest of new lives"* (John 12:24 NLT).

The death of Jesus gives us life (see Gal. 2:20; Rom. 6:4-5), just as a new kernel of corn gets life from the death of the original kernel. Paul explains, *"I declare to you the gospel…that Christ died for our sins… and that He was buried and that He rose again the third day according to the Scriptures"* (1 Cor. 15:1-4).

I first encountered this death principle in February 1951. My roommate at Columbia Bible College was Ed Tripp. He first died spiritually (see Gal. 2:20) as a Merchant Marine during World War II when someone led him to Jesus Christ. Then he graduated from the University of Nebraska and enrolled at Columbia Bible College to study missions in the graduate school.

On many occasions, I prayed around our dormitory beds with Ed and two other roommates. And what do I remember of Ed? He was dedicated, obedient, and glorified God in all that he did.

Ed left Columbia around Christmastime in 1950 to go to a primitive unevangelized tribe in New Guinea. He planned to minister among the unevangelized Indian tribes to reach them for Jesus Christ. He, along with Walter Erikson, were chopped to death with machetes as they slept at night by those they went to reach. The military flew in on helicopters, found their bodies, and buried them in the jungle.

Years later, a helicopter flew into the same jungle and lowered a granite stone near their graves, commemorating the death of Ed and Walter, who died as Christian martyrs.

In the spring of 2017, I preached at Columbia Bible College and told this story, asking the following question: *Why did Ed and Walter die and I was left alive?* George Murray, former president of Columbia Bible College, got up to answer my question. He told of flying in a small Missionary Aviation Fellowship plane into that area of the New Guinea jungle. Surrounding the airstrip were over 2,000 native believers beating drums and singing "Hallelujah" praises to God. A missionary couple from Columbia Bible College took Ed's place, and as a result, over 20,000 believers from that region are members of the church of Jesus Christ today. There are three Bible institutes there today; one is called the "Erikson-Tritt Theological College." The kernel of wheat that fell into the ground died. And from that martyr's death has come a massive church of believers who give praise and glory to Jesus Christ.

THE CHURCH BEGINS WITH JESUS

This book is about *planting reproducing churches.*[2] Why plant churches? And why is it important? What is the urgency of church planting, and where does it all begin? Technically, everything goes back to Jesus. Christianity begins with the invitation of Jesus. *"Come unto Me..."* (Matt. 11:28 KJV).

Therefore, salvation is coming to Jesus Christ. This experience is also called believing in Christ, receiving Christ, or following Christ. Didn't He say, *"Follow Me, and I will make you...fishers of men"* (Mark 1:17)?

Everything about the life of Jesus points to His death on the cross because it was there He died for the sins of the world. Previously, a Jew had to come to the temple bringing a sacrificial lamb, which a priest would then offer for atonement. But Jesus' death changed everything. *"Behold! The Lamb of God who takes away the sin of the world!"* (John 1:29). Notice it was not just for the sins of Israel, but for the world.

But more importantly than His death is His resurrection. On the third day, Jesus rose from the dead to give new life to those who follow Him. It wasn't enough to have sins forgiven; His followers now have new life—eternal life—which is the life of God living in them.

THE GREAT COMMISSION: GOD'S STRATEGY[3]

How was the message of Jesus' death going to be spread to all the world? Jesus rose from the dead early Sunday morning and appeared to a group of women, then later to Peter, Mary Magdalene, and a couple walking home to Emmaus. Later that evening, ten disciples were gathered in the Upper Room for fear of the Jews. Protecting one's self was natural. They thought that because the Jews had executed Jesus, the Jews were looking to kill them also. The doors were locked. Other than that, the Upper Room was a comfortable place because the disciples had met with Jesus in the same room for the Last Supper on Thursday evening.

"Peace be unto you..." is the first thing Jesus said when He appeared to them (John 20:21 KJV). Fearful hearts need peace. The last thing Jesus said in that same Upper Room on Thursday evening was, *"Peace I leave with you, My peace I give to you..."* (John 14:27). Great words of encouragement.

Jesus showed the disciples the wounds in His hands and side. This was proof that He was the same Jesus. As the Bible says, *"...He showed them His hands and His side. Then the disciples were glad when they saw the Lord"* (John 20:20). The Bible word for *saw* suggests that they touched and examined His wounds carefully. Then Jesus gives them a command of authority and destiny: *"...As the Father has sent Me, so I am sending you"* (John 20:21 NLT). This is a command to *go*. Notice what Jesus did not command. He did not tell them where to go, what to do when they got there, nor what to speak... nothing.

What He wanted was their unconditional obedience. So He commanded, "Go..."

The second giving of the Great Commission occurred a week later. Disciples were again in the Upper Room, except this time there were 11 disciples. Thomas—the doubting disciple—had originally run away further and hidden deeper than any other disciple. So he was not in the Upper Room that first Sunday evening. But Thomas was now present the second Sunday.

When Thomas finally came out of hiding, the disciples told him they saw Jesus and His wounds. But Thomas always doubted, so he boldly exclaimed, *"Except I place my fingers into His wounds, and thrust my fist into His side, I will not believe"* (John 20:25 ELT). It's terrible to tell God you will not believe, but that was evidence of Thomas's doubtful heart. Jesus invited Thomas to put his fingers into the wounds of His hands and thrust his fist into His side. Then He added the challenge, *"...be not faithless, but believing"* (John 20:27 KJV).

The Bible does not tell us what Thomas did, but most think he did not accept Jesus' invitation to examine His wounds. Instead he fell worshiping Jesus and exclaimed, *"My Lord and my God"* (John 20:28 KJV). This is the highest expression of Old Testament deity. Thomas declared that Jesus is not only the Creator God, but also the Lord of the universe.

That evening, Jesus gave the second part of the Great Commission: *"Go into all the world and preach the Good News to everyone"* (Mark 16:15 NLT). Notice carefully, Jesus did not exclude Gentiles, nor did He only include Jews. Jesus said to go everywhere and preach to everyone.

Jesus' strategy changed everything. God had focused His work on the Jews in the Old Testament; they were His people, and from them would come priests, kings, prophets, the Old Testament, and eventually the Messiah. Jesus Christ had come from the Jews. But this command had a totally new focus. It would take some time for them to understand this expanded command.

The second giving of the Great Commission had an unlimited distinction, "the world," and an unlimited audience, "everyone."

The third giving of the Great Commission occurred either three or four weeks after the resurrection. The disciples gathered on a mountain in Galilee, probably near Capernaum. This could have been the Mount of the Beatitudes or the mountain where Jesus fed the 5,000. The Book of First Corinthians suggests there were 500 people when He appeared on this occasion (see 1 Cor. 15:6).

This time, Jesus included a strategy in the Great Commission: *"Go therefore and make disciples of all the nations [ethne, people groups] baptizing them…teaching them to observe all things that I have commanded you"* (Matt. 28:19-20). This third command included more than a directive to announce or preach the Gospel to all people. Now Jesus wants them to get results. Those who heard their preaching would believe, then they were to be baptized, and then they too would be discipled or taught to obey the commands Jesus taught them. Do you see "reproduction" in this command?

These new followers of Jesus would come from all ethnic groups or people groups of the world. They would be assembled by baptism and the teaching of the Word of God.

It is interesting that this command instructed, "Make disciples of all people groups." Did Jesus mean to focus on the people in these ethnic groups, or did He mean to bring His influence into the culture of these groups so that the Gospel would change their culture or way of life? He meant both!

When Jesus said, *"baptizing them,"* He meant they were to formally induct new followers into their fellowship. These new believers were to identify with Jesus Christ spiritually but also with each other physically in water. These new believers would be identified with the assembly (the church). Jesus could be read here as saying to congregationalize all new converts.

By teaching all new converts all things, they would obey what Jesus commanded them. This third giving of the Great Commission indicated that they were to preach to lost people, get them saved, then baptize them and gather them into a local assembly. It suggested creating a new *strategy*, that is, planting reproducing churches.

The fourth giving of the Great Commission happened 40 days after Jesus' death. Jesus and His disciples were in Jerusalem, where He clarified the content of the Gospel message. They would not instruct followers to come to Jerusalem as the Old Testament commands, nor would they instruct people to bring a sacrificial lamb to the priest for atonement. Jesus taught them to preach His death, burial, and resurrection. *"That is how it was written, and that is why it was inevitable that Christ should suffer, and rise from the dead on the third day. So must the change of heart which leads to the forgiveness of sins be proclaimed in His name to all nations..."* (Luke 24:46-47 PHILLIPS).

This fourth giving of the Great Commission explains the *message* that must be preached to all ethnic groups in the world. The heart of the Gospel message is now the death, burial, and resurrection of Jesus Christ (see 1 Cor. 15:1-5).

The fifth giving of the Great Commission happened later on that fortieth day, and it involved *geography*. The disciples left the city of Jerusalem to walk to the Mount of Olives. The disciples were probably not sure what their commission involved, because they asked, *"Will You at this time restore the kingdom...?"* (Acts 1:6). Jesus told them it was not for them to know the times and seasons when the Kingdom would be coming. He focused their attention on the original giving of the Great Commission: *"...you will be My witnesses, telling people about Me everywhere—in Jerusalem, throughout Judea, and Samaria, and to the ends of the earth"* (Acts 1:8 NLT). This command included *geography*. They were to begin in Jerusalem, that is, the city where they were located. When the Great Commission was given to later generations, they were to begin in "their Jerusalem." Each person's Jerusalem is the place where they met Christ, prayed, and the Holy Spirit came upon them. From their home base, they are to reach out geographically into the whole world.

HOW WAS JESUS' COMMAND CARRIED OUT?[4]

Simple Arithmetic

Three miraculous signs appeared to the disciples praying in the Upper Room (the sound of a loud wind, multiple tongues of fire coming on each person, and each person speaking a different tongue/language). The miraculous signs attracted a huge crowd. They began questioning the disciples about the obvious supernatural phenomena. Then Peter stood up to preach the new Gospel message of the death, burial, and resurrection of Jesus Christ.

How did each hearer understand the Gospel in their own language? Because those praying in the Upper Room had been given the gift of tongues, or foreign languages, each one began interpreting Peter's message to an audience in the language they understood. When Peter began preaching, people of the same language gathered together into a cluster, and each person heard the Gospel in their own tongue.

That gift of tongues was a future prediction of what would happen, as the Gospel would be preached around the world. Each person could hear and understand. God's plan from the beginning has been for each person to hear within their own language, with the understanding of their culture.

Because the crowd on Pentecost was convicted of their sins, they cried, *"...what shall we do?"* (Acts 2:37). Peter responded, *"Repent..."* (Acts 2:38). What were the results?

"There were added unto them about three thousand..." (Acts 2:41 KJV). Do you see the word *added*? The early church began to grow by simple arithmetic. The 120 praying in the Upper Room became 3,120.

Compounded Growth

A short time later, as Peter and John were going into the temple, they healed a crippled man. That led to another sermon by Peter. Again, a number of people believed the Gospel of Jesus Christ, the result being that *"...the number of men came to be about five thousand"* (Acts 4:4). The Greek word here is *males*. This is probably a reference to the Book of Numbers, where Jews only counted the head of the household, that is, men. The early church followed that numbering practice. That means there were about 5,000 men, plus their wives, plus 2 to 3 children per family. The early church must have had 20,000 to 25,000 people.

Its opposition accused them, *"You have filled all of Jerusalem with your teaching about Him..."* (Acts 5:28 NLT). It wasn't just the preaching of Peter; it was everyone preaching to all, at all times and in all places. This verse has described saturation evangelism: "using every available means to reach every available person at every available time."[5]

Multiplication Growth

Next, a more intensive arithmetic word is used to describe the early church growth, that is, *multiply*. *"The believers rapidly multiplied..."* (Acts 6:1 NLT).

Adding is simple growth, for example, 10 + 10. But multiplication leads to unlimited growth, for example, 20 x 20. This reference to multiplication probably is a reference to the command God gave the first parents, *"Multiply..."* (Gen. 1:26 ELT).

Exponential Multiplication

The next use of the arithmetic phrase applies to churches, not just individuals: *"The churches...were multiplied"* (Acts 9:31). The early church was doing what Jesus had commanded—not only getting people saved, but baptizing them and getting them into congregations. When that happened, churches multiplied.

But in addition to individual salvation, Jesus suggested influencing their culture: *"...make disciples of all the nations..."* (Matt. 28:19). This probably did not mean to "Christianize" the culture but to influence the way people lived, which would influence culture. When the church got to Corinth, it was accused of doing it: *"These who have turned the world upside down have come here too"* (Acts 17:6).

HOW IS AMERICA FULFILLING THE GREAT COMMISSION?[6]

According to the best statistics available, approximately 80 percent of all American churches have plateaued or are declining in numbers. They are not adding or multiplying. They are stagnant. (See Cchapter 2 for information about the growth of Christianity in the Global South and the Oriental Crescent, while Western Christianity is stagnant).

The same statistics suggest that approximately 10 percent of churches are adding believers. That means they are focusing on preaching the Gospel to individuals, which is the first part of the Great Commission.

Again, the statistics indicate that about 4 percent of Americans are actively planting another church like their own. This is described as *adding churches*. While 4 percent is significant, did not God intend for all of His churches to multiply?

Finally, approximately 1 percent of American churches are multiplying. That means they are planting churches that reproduce other churches (see Acts 9:31).

Very little multiple church planting is happening in the United States, yet this is the strategy used in the rapid growth of the church in the Global South and the Oriental Crescent. Those churches are growing because they are fulfilling the command to "multiply" and they are doing it by planting multiple churches.

GOD'S NEXT EVANGELISTIC METHOD[7]

God uses different methods to communicate His message to people. Some heard the audible Word of God like Noah, Abraham, Isaac, and Jacob, and certain succeeding leaders.

Then God's presence descended on Mount Sinai, where He talked to Moses face to face (see Exod. 19). God laid out the basic directions for all of mankind in the Ten Commandments. Moses saw God's manifestations, and God spoke to him; and through him, God spoke to the people.

Next, God raised up prophets called "seers" (see 1 Sam. 9:9). God spoke to them through visions, dreams, and audible communicators. Prophets spoke God's Word to the people; sometimes they communicated His message through symbolic acts (Ezekiel and Jeremiah).

After Jesus rose from the dead, He sent His disciples to preach to every person in the world and make disciples of all nations (cultures) (see Mark 16:15; Matt. 28:19). This meant to congregationalize them into assemblies by baptism, *"teaching them to obey all things that* [Jesus had] *taught* [them]" (Matt. 28:20 ELT).

The early church spread the message of the Gospel everywhere Christians went. Churches sprang up that consolidated its gains, then trained and empowered disciples to convert other lost people and baptize them into new churches.

Over the centuries, Christians have attempted to carry out the Great Commission in their personal ministry to lost people. And collectively through the church, they have used a variety of methods to evangelize lost people. Some methods have been more effective than others. The church has used some of the following evangelistic methods: street preaching, literature (tract) evangelism, media (radio, television) evangelism, local church evangelistic crusades, great interchurch evangelistic crusades (for example, Billy Graham's crusades), Sunday school bus evangelism, seeker church evangelism, etc. The different methods of evangelism could be expanded, but none is as effective as church-planting evangelism.

But in recent times, we have seen the explosion of Christianity in the Global South and the Oriental Crescent. Churches in these areas were originally reached through many evangelistic methods used by Western Christianity, namely, cross-cultural evangelism.[8] Every child, like every church, must take over for their aging parents, standing on their shoulders, reaching higher, doing more, and accomplishing miracles for God. So the "new" churches around the world are standing on the shoulders of Western Christianity and doing more for God. The greatest growth in Christianity in the past 50 years has been in the Global South and the Oriental Crescent.[9] This explosion of Christianity is greater than the original Protestant Reformation initiated by Martin Luther in the fifteenth century that laid the foundation for Western Christianity.[10]

Although Christian churches in the Global South and the Oriental Crescent have learned many lessons from Western Christianity, they are using a new methodology that is nothing more than a return to the original Christianity of the early church. The extensive church planting by indigenous churches in the Global South and the

Oriental Crescent has contributed to the explosive growth of Christianity in those regions.

ANALYSIS OF CHURCH PLANTING METHODS

This new movement of church planting has several expressions. Yes, church planting is planting new congregations! But there are several methods used to plant new churches. Here is a suggested list, but it is not complete:

1. Planting new churches by multisite church expansion—one mother church planting many satellite churches but keeping all congregations together for mutual strength, mutual outreach, and mutual discipleship.

2. One church planting another independent church.

3. Agency church planting (denominational or interdenominational cooperation).

4. The house church movement.

5. A mother church with home cells.

6. One church planting media churches.

This new church planting movement is not new. When the early church carried out the Great Commission, they did it with church planting. Everywhere early Christians went (by choice or persecution), they witnessed Jesus Christ's power in their lives; and as a result, new churches were born or planted.

They didn't go to plant churches, but as a result of their going, new churches were assembled. When they won new believers to the Lord, they baptized them. Then they assembled them together to teach them to obey all that Christ had taught them. They fellowshipped together, prayed together, and ministered together. Their

Christian life had dramatic growth, and one of the results was a new church. They didn't go out primarily to plant a new church; they went to talk about Jesus everywhere they could. And isn't a church the assembly of Jesus with His people?

Around the world today, the church is the focus of the Great Commission—not the primary focus, but you cannot carry out the Great Commission without planting churches.

SIX CHURCH PLANTING METHODS FROM AROUND THE WORLD

The following list is not arranged in order of importance or by strength of the church planting method. It is not even in historical order. And beyond that, it is not a complete list. There are other ways of planting a church, but this list includes those that have current visibility.

1. *Planting New Churches by Multisite Church Expansion*

Perhaps the greatest picture of church planting is the Jotabeche Church in Santiago, Chile, which was started in 1911.[11] This church grew out of the influence of the Azusa Street Revival in California. The Jotabeche Church is a multisite church (one central location and many satellite churches) with branches across the city of Santiago, Chile. The main street location is the Cathedral in central Santiago, which seated 19,000 people 40 years ago (today it seats 14,000). There are about 20 temples surrounding the city seating from 200 to 2,000 each. Next, there are over 80 churches, averaging up to 400 in attendance. In addition, there is an abundance of Sunday school missions, each one planted to become a church and/or temple.

The Jotabeche Church has had only one pastor at a time over the years, with lay preachers in each temple and church. All believers are members of the mother church and take communion only once a year on Good Friday at the central location. Visiting groups from surrounding temples and churches populate the huge Sunday night crusades. Originally, the church was known for its giant parades that walked through the streets, inviting visitors to go with them to the central church for a great Sunday evening celebration.

Now there are multiple Jotabeche churches scattered throughout Chile in most of the major metropolitan areas. The Santiago church has around 140,000 members combined in the Cathedral, temples, and churches. But there are over five million believers in all of the Jotabeche (multisite) churches throughout Chile.

The multisite church movement is found in many other denominations and independent churches around the world, and the movement is beginning to appear in the United Sates (see Chapter 7).

2. One Church Planting Other Independent Churches

The Bethany Church in Surabaya, Indonesia, is affiliated with the Church of God (Cleveland, Tennessee) and has multiple services each Sunday.[12] Because of the growth of the Bethany Church, Pastor Alex said to me, "There are more Pentecostals in Indonesia than any other nation in the world."[13] This one church has planted a network of over 700 churches throughout the islands of Indonesia. In a nation that is heavily influenced by Islam, the Gospel of Jesus Christ is not forced underground. This is amazing considering Indonesia has the fifth largest population in the world and has more Muslims than any other nation.

3. Agency Church Planting (Denominational and Interdenominational)

The World Harvest Church in Suva, Fiji, is a single church with 4,000 weekly worshipers.[14] Originally, Pastor Suliasi Kurulo was an engineer who worked for the government. He began knocking on doors on a smaller island to win people to Christ. He eventually began a church and together with his church went to every door on their island witnessing for Christ. Then he planted a couple more churches. However, with a passion for all the 300-plus inhabited islands of Fiji, he moved to Suva, that nation's capital, and began another church, the World Harvest Center, and planned to knock on every door on all the islands of Fiji. Through the World Harvest Center, he has planted multiple churches on every island of Fiji, some of which have at least ten churches. Then his vision motivated him to plant churches on other islands in the Pacific Ocean and the Indian Ocean, as well as churches in Central and South America, with a total of over 6,500 churches. His goal: plant over 100,000 churches.

Suliasi says, "If you stick a pin through the center of the earth at Jerusalem, the pin comes out at Fiji, 'the ends of the earth.'" His motto is "From the ends of the earth, to the rest of the earth."[15]

4. Planting House Churches

The house church movement in China is located almost everywhere in the country, but almost no one knows how to find one. Without advertisements, sanctuaries or buildings, or any type of publicity, the Chinese house church (also known as the underground church) has become one of the most powerful Christian movements in the world.[16] Without denominational support or strategy, the movement continues to grow supernaturally.

Unofficially, there are more than 130 million believers in China. While there is an official Three-Self Church in China, with a registration of approximately 23.5 million members, almost 100 million people assemble in house churches in homes, apartments, restaurants, and other places. Observers suggest there were no underground churches in 1949 when the Communists took over China, yet today Christianity has exploded in this country of 1.5 billion people. China represents one-fifth of the world's population, and its government is considered unfriendly, if not hostile, to Christianity. The house church movement has grown without the aid of foreign mission-ary groups, organized structure, programs, or influence from outside nations.

5. A Mother Church with Home Cells

The Yoido Full Gospel Church has grown through home cells throughout the city of Seoul, South Korea, and has become, with over 760,000 believers, the largest church in history. David Yonggi Cho founded the church in 1958, and it rapidly grew to more than 3,000 in attendance. Cho had a heart attack while baptizing one Sunday after the third Sunday morning service in the 2,400-seat auditorium. He then realized he could not pastor or build the church on his own strength.

During his recuperation, Cho came up with a strategy to use small home cells, placed strategically in every part of the city, to reach and nurture people for Jesus Christ. Each cell would be an extension of his church where the Word of God was taught and peo-ple worshiped God, prayed, fellowshipped, and spoke in tongues as evidence of the baptism of the Holy Spirit. By 1978, Cho had reached 100,000 people, and the church was growing exponentially. By 2008, when Cho retired, the church had reached 760,000 in attendance, with 32,000 small groups and 50 satellite locations throughout the city and in other areas.[17]

The secret of its growth was the continuous addition of home cells. Cho stated, "Just as the physical body grows by the division of cells, so the local church body grows by the division of cells."[18]

6. One Church Planting Media Churches

Glory of Zion International Ministries in Corinth, Texas, has 1,500 worshipers in residence each weekend but includes another 30,000 who worship online.[19] All worshipers also minister to one another via the Internet. All come into the church through a membership class taught online. When Pastor Chuck Pierce baptizes a new believer in water in Corinth, Texas, other new members are baptized at the same time around the world. The same unity is experienced with the Lord's Table.

Chuck Pierce planted this church in Denton, Texas, then later added Internet outreach in 2004. This church includes 5,000 Internet house churches, each with a leader-shepherd who oversees a group of believers who gather to view the Sunday services on their computers. The house church averages between 2 and 25 believers (more than a biological family). While some Internet churches claim a larger viewership, this church is influential because viewers have made a commitment-vow to the church through a membership class, have become regular financial givers, and pray for one another and with one another through the Internet.[20]

Another Internet church is Life.Church, which is based out of Oklahoma City, Oklahoma. It has 16 campuses in cities around the United States and more than 50 viewing times via the Internet in most time zones.[21] Craig Groeschel is the founding pastor (1994), and the other innovative leader is Bobby Gruenewald. The church's Internet outreach is similar to a church media ministry, while Glory of Zion attempts to tie its members into community worship and outreach ministry.

Christ Fellowship in Palm Beach Gardens, Florida, another leader in Internet churches, has a large Internet outreach with more than 20,000 views weekly. Todd Mullins is the pastor. The church counts loyalty by the amount of offerings received, which is around four dollars per viewer.[22]

CONCLUSION

Wherever early Christians went, either because of choice or because of persecution, they attested to Jesus Christ's power in their lives. Because of this, new churches were born or planted.

They didn't go to plant churches, but as a result of their going, new churches were assembled. When they won new believers to the Lord, they baptized them. Their Christian life had dramatic growth, and one of the results was a new church. They didn't go out primarily to plant a new church; they went to talk about Jesus everywhere they could. And isn't a church the assembly of Jesus with His people?

Around the world today, church planting is one of the ways that the Great Commission is being completed. It's not the only focus, but you cannot carry out the Great Commission without planting churches.

CHAPTER 2

WHAT IS GOD DOING IN THE WORLD?

The biggest movement of God in the world today is church planting. Some have claimed it is God's newest or latest method of evangelism. That means the church is coming back to the most effective evangelism method of the past. However, this movement of church planting is not coming primarily from Western Christianity; it is coming from the Global South and the Oriental Crescent.

This church planting movement is largely coming from the Global South (Africa, Latin America, Indonesia, and India) and the Oriental Crescent (China and South Korea).[1] This is a shift in momentum from the past, when traditional Western nations, that is, the United States, Europe, Australia, and New Zealand, were leaders in church growth.

This shift is mostly ignored by mainstream media, but the statistics show that evangelical Christianity is growing elsewhere, not in the United States, Britain, and Europe. This growth is in nations that were not traditionally Christian. In many cases, the cultures of these countries are hostile to the evangelical church, or at least they were not friendly to evangelical church expansion and/or planting.

NATION/REGION CULTURAL OPPOSITION TO EVANGELICALISM	
Africa	Heathenism
South and Central America	Roman Catholicism
Indonesia	Islam
India	Hinduism
China	Communism
South Korea	Buddhism

In the past 50 years, the political world has been divided into the West (the United States, Britain, and Europe), the East (Russia and Communist Bloc nations), and the Third World (sometimes called the "undeveloped nations"). These were primarily political divisions, but they also were based on economic, social, and ethnic distinctions, helping people to understand the differences in how people lived and ruled themselves in various parts of the world.

However, today we can divide the Christian world into two general areas: Western Christianity is represented by the United States, Britain, Europe, Canada, and nations that reflect Western culture, such as Australia, and New Zealand. Global Christianity comprises Global South (Africa, South America, Indonesia, Malaysia, India) and the Oriental Crescent (China and South Korea).

We can quickly summarize these two areas of Christianity. The church in the Global South and the Oriental Crescent is growing in size, strength, and vibrancy. Western Christianity, on the other hand, is in maintenance mode; it's hanging on to its gains made in past centuries.

A century ago, this was not the case. In 1910, about two-thirds of the world's Christians lived in Europe, where the bulk of Christians had been for a millennium, according to estimates by the Center for the Study of Global Christianity.[2] Today, only about a quarter of all Christians live in Europe (26 percent). A plurality—more than a third—now are in the Americas (37 percent). About one in every four Christians lives in sub-Saharan Africa (24 percent), and about one in eight is found in Asia and the Pacific (13 percent).[3]

Four years ago, my wife passed away, and at the same time I retired from the position of Dean of Liberty University's School of Religion and Liberty Baptist Theological Seminary. That freed me up to travel. As a result, I visited 20 foreign nations, usually invited by indigenous groups from each nation. I did not travel under the umbrella of Western Christianity or American foreign missions or sending agencies. I experienced the church's growth, vitality, and developing denominational governance through their eyes, not through Western eyes. From this experience, I have drawn certain conclusions about what God is doing in the world.

Then I began researching the latest articles, books, and reports from those gathering data, observing trends, and reporting what's happening around the world. The vitality of Christianity is no longer in Western Christianity; rather, it is in the Global South and the Oriental Crescent. However, Western Christianity still considers itself superior to the rest of the world and expects all cultures to reflect its standards, vision, and values. It expects the churches of the world to look like Western churches. But they don't; they reflect the culture where the Gospel has been planted.

Now we must deal with the fact that secular and Christian media have not recognized the vitality of Christianity in the Global South and the Oriental Crescent. They look at these countries through Western eyes. They think these nations are poor and impoverished and need the help of Western churches. Also, they see cultural barriers in each nation and view Christianity's task as cross-cultural, which means they began with a negative approach, that is, "We can't do evangelism in our comfortable way; we must adapt and do it another way." America approaches the world through cross-cultural evangelism. Finally, Western media think other cultures are inferior to Western culture so they attempt to conform foreign Christianity to Western Christian culture. Western Christianity wants foreign churches to preach with Western formats, be organized by Western business practices, and live by Western cultural standards. But they don't want that.

Philip Jenkins, professor at Baylor University and author of *The Next Christendom: The Coming of Global Christianity*, writes, "Much of the story of Christianity outside of Western Christianity is told in terms of conflict over doctrine and issues. The Western media has neglected its strength, accomplishments, and victories."[4]

For the most part, Western Christianity considers the social economic and cultural issues of the Bible to be foreign or irrelevant to the non-Westerner. But at the same time, the Global South understands these biblical issues from a social and cultural aspect, and they accept and follow the authority of Scripture in these areas.

Global South churches engage in healing, deliverance, and spiritual warfare, practices not typically found in Western Christianity. Western Christianity uses these terms in its vocabulary but does not seek to practice them—and if it does, it does so in symbolic gestures only.

Western Christianity, or at least Western media, is most concerned with social injustice and emphasizes racism, feminism, sexism, and economic elitism. But the West does not focus on the social issues of healing; deliverance from physical, mental, and emotional bondage; or spiritual victory over evil.

Churches in the Global South feel that regeneration and the power of God are the starting points for social justice. As a note, the Global South sees liberation, deliverance, and victory as a spiritual basis, not a political and/or economical basis. Some even think that Global South Christianity is doing a better job by internal transformation of culture than the West is doing by external political pressure. Rather than top-down from the government by legislation, the transformation is coming from the bottom up, that is, from the people first, who then influence government and legislature. This is an inside-out transformation.

Western Christianity tends to focus evangelism on media (television, radio, mass distribution, and social media), emphasizing persuasion evangelism (from the outside in). Western churches use advertising to attract seekers, invite people, and/or communicate their music and spiritual experience to bring people to Christ. As a result, the main thrust of Western Christianity is bringing people to Christ the way that Coca-Cola or Mercedes Benz markets and sells their products. The primary thrust of the Global South is relationship evangelism and/or family evangelism, which has an internal appeal from the inside out.

A traditional emphasis of Western Christianity is doctrine, each group accentuating its beliefs, communicating them, and standing in its strength. However, Western Christianity does not realize that doctrine divides. Global Christianity places emphasis on the Person of Jesus Christ. He unites and brings people together, while doctrine can do the opposite. The primary source of Western Christianity's strength and resources is its finances.

We are living through one of the greatest ages of change in the history of Christianity…wider, and faster than the era of the

Reformation itself...change, producing tumult and turbulence as a sign of growth, health and birth.[5]

STRENGTH AND GROWTH IN AFRICA

There has been a massive surge of Christianity in Africa. As *Wikipedia* states:

> There has been tremendous growth in the number of Christians in Africa—coupled by a relative decline in adherence to traditional African religions. Only nine million Christians were in Africa in 1900, but by the year 2000, there were an estimated 380 million Christians. According to a 2006 Pew Forum on Religion and Public Life study, 147 million African Christians were "renewalists" (Pentecostals and Charismatics). According to David Barrett, most of the 552,000 congregations in 11,500 denominations throughout Africa in 1995 are completely unknown in the West. Much of the recent Christian growth in Africa is now due to African evangelism rather than European missionaries.[6]

Christianity has spread in southern African nations, southeast African nations, and central African nations. The Coptic Church of Egypt (a wing of the Eastern Orthodox Church) is a significant minority in Egypt. The *World Book Encyclopedia* estimates that in 2002, approximately 80 percent of Africans were Christians (the other 20 percent being Muslims).[7]

One of the strongest movements is the Born Again Pentecostal Church of Uganda, who reports online approximately 22,000 churches.[8] However, when I visited Entebbe, Uganda, in 2015, I talked with former Bishop P. Alex Milala, General Overseer. He served two terms, and during that time, 8,000 new congregations were planted. I have heard him lecture about "how to begin a 'grass hut' church that motivated listeners to go to it with android power," that is, learning church planting through the cell phone.

STRENGTH AND GROWTH IN SOUTH AND CENTRAL AMERICA

In the summer of 1982, I toured five nations in South America looking for the largest churches in the world. John Maxwell and John Vaughan went with me. Eventually, I wrote an article titled "The World's Ten Largest Churches."[9] I was amazed to find megachurches (churches with an attendance of 1,000 or more) that were unknown outside their denominational and geographical borders. I estimated there were 50 megachurches in all of South America. Today, I would estimate that there are 5,000 megachurches there.

> Especially since the 1960s, the region has witnessed dramatic growth in the number of Pentecostals. According to 2005 figures from the World Christian Database, Pentecostals represent 13%, or about 75 million, of Latin America's population of nearly 560 million. Charismatic members of non-Pentecostal denominations, who in Latin America are overwhelmingly Catholic, number an additional 80 million or so, or 15% of the population.[10]

I was amazed at the size and strength of the Pentecostals in South America. Even though I was hosted in every country by Southern Baptist missionaries, they took me to Pentecostal churches.

Pentecostals represent the most rapidly growing sector of Latin American Protestantism. For example, in Brazil, which has by far the region's largest Protestant population in absolute terms, the national census shows that Pentecostals grew from less than 50% of Protestants in 1980 to 68% in 2000. In Central America, Pentecostals grew from 37% of Protestants in 1965 to more than half by the 1980s (Freston 2004a: 228). Today, according to the World Christian Database, Pentecostals make up some 73% of all Latin American Protestants.[11]

Besides various denominational and interdenominational missionary works in South and Central America, there have been other evangelistic endeavors that have made an impact on the region. First, there were the giant open-air evangelistic crusades by Jimmy Swaggart and other Pentecostal/Charismatic leaders. Finally, there were the giant open-air crusades of Billy Graham.

Then came the massive in-depth evangelism campaign by Ken Strachan, president of Latin American Mission in the late 1950s and 1960s. He challenged all Protestant mission agencies to (1) develop a nationwide strategy, (2) reach every area (culture) of each country, (3) bring the churches together in evangelism to penetrate every aspect of culture (he advocated a bottom-up evangelistic strategy using the unknown evangelist and musicians, not a top-down strategy that began with internationally known evangelists and nationally known Christian musicians in a big arena), and (4) develop a view of presenting Christ to every person in every country.

C. Peter Wagner was president of Bolivian Indian Mission at the time and organized the Bolivar Church for In-Depth Evangelism. Yet after a year of interdenominational church evangelism, he was confused with the results. Even though many had professed Christ publicly (at least made a decision), the base membership of every church group had gone down, not up. It was this experience that focused Wagner's emphasis on local church growth, not crusade evangelism or confrontational evangelism. He came to the conclusion that interdenominational or interchurch evangelism could get decisions, but it didn't prepare disciples (the mandate of Matthew 28:20), nor did it grow churches. That experience caused Wagner to devote the rest of his life to teaching the principles of church growth at Fuller Theological Seminary in Pasadena, California. Perhaps this conclusion found its way to the church at large in Central and South America.

The impact of Pentecostalism on Latin America's religious landscape has been profound. It has led, for example, to a dramatic increase in the number of Pentecostal churches in important urban centers. A major 1992 survey of religious institutions in the Greater Rio area of Brazil found that 61% of all existing churches were Pentecostal. It also found that this proportion was rapidly increasing, with Pentecostal churches accounting for roughly nine-in-ten congregations registered in the preceding two years (1990-1992). In one Catholic diocese in Greater Rio, Protestant places of worship outnumbered Catholic ones by two-to-one, and in the poorest districts the ratio climbs to almost seven-to-one (Freston 2004a: 231).[12]

Pentecostal churches have led the growth of Christianity in Latin America. Pentecostalism is a branch of Protestant Christianity, but it is growing more rapidly than non-Pentecostal Protestantism.

In 2010, I spoke to 8,000 pastors in Argentina for Ed Silvoso, who leads Harvest Evangelism and who was the foremost leader of the Argentinian revival.[13] He instituted what is called *marketplace evangelism* (evangelism that includes businesses, educational institutions, and government). He also was the first to use the idea of *prayer walking*, that is, "praying on site with insight."[14] Massive churches have grown in Argentina, and the movement has spread all over the world. A recent book by Hans Geir Aasmundsen, *Pentecostals, Politics, and Religious Equality in Argentina*, claims that Pentecostals represent over 10 percent of the population.[15]

Tens of millions of Latin Americans have left the Roman Catholic Church in recent decades and embraced Pentecostal Christianity, according to a new Pew Research Center survey on religion in 18 Latin American countries and Puerto Rico. Indeed, nearly one-in-five Latin Americans now describe themselves as Protestant, and across the countries surveyed majorities of them self-identify as Pentecostal or belong to a Pentecostal denomination. Pentecostals share many beliefs with other evangelical Protestants, but they put more emphasis on the "gifts of the Holy Spirit," such as speaking in tongues, faith healing, and prophesying.[16]

In Chapter 1, you were introduced to the Jotabeche Church in Santiago, Chile, affiliated with the Pentecostal Holiness Church of America.[17] It is a multisite church with affiliated temples, churches, and Sunday school missions. The huge church in Santiago is duplicated in other large cities in Chile with a nationwide membership of over five million members.

STRENGTH AND GROWTH IN INDONESIA

Alex Tanuseputra founded the Graha Bethany Nginden megachurch in 1977. The present auditorium is the same type of aluminum dome used at Liberty University (my home), except that there are two balconies and several "fingers" of expanded seating, which Liberty doesn't have. Liberty seats 10,000 by count, and Bethany seats 25,000 (I counted them in 2008). The church is affiliated with the International Church of God (Cleveland, Tennessee). Pastor Alex told me there are several worship services on Sunday with an attendance of over 140,000. He also has planted 700 churches on the various islands of

Indonesia. I spoke to a group of 8,000 pastors at a "unity" service representing many Protestant denominations. It was there I learned of the growth of Pentecostalism in Indonesia. Alex claimed, "There are more Pentecostals in Indonesia than in any other nation of the world."[18]

In Indonesia, a country with a Muslim majority, Pentecostal/ Charismatic churches are growing in urban contexts. Young people especially are attracted by the living worship of the Pentecostal/Charismatic churches, organized very professionally with an integration of multimedia, music, decor, and lighting. The pop and rock music is most attractive, in combination with the sermons of the pastors, which are simple and near to the daily life experiences, showing how Jesus is near to everybody, giving comfort, forgiveness, healing, direction, and even material prosperity and happiness.[19]

This is an amazing fact considering that Indonesia has the world's largest Islamic population (Indonesia is the fourth largest in total population).[20]

More surprising, though, is the boom in Christianity—officially Indonesia's second largest faith and a growing force throughout Asia. Indeed, the number of Asian Christian faithful exploded to 351 million adherents in 2005, up from 101 million in 1970, according to the *Pew Research Center on* Religion and Public Life, based in Washington, D.C.[21]

STRENGTH AND GROWTH IN CHINA

Today there are an estimated 100 million members of the house church movement (the underground church), with about 23 million in the Three-Self Church, which is the church registered with the Communist government.[22]

China's Protestant community, which had just one million members in 1949, has already overtaken those of countries more commonly associated with an evangelical boom. In 2010, there were more than 58 million Protestants in China compared to 40 million in Brazil and 36 million in South Africa, according to the Pew Research Centre's Forum on Religion and Public Life. Professor Yang, a leading expert on religion in China, believes that number will swell to around 160 million by 2025. That would likely put China ahead even of the United States, which had around 159 million Protestants in 2010 but whose congregations are in decline.

By 2030, China's total Christian population, including Catholics, would exceed 247 million, placing it above Mexico, Brazil, and the United States as the largest Christian congregation in the world, he predicted.[23]

The conversion rate in China is high. Many are becoming believers in both house churches and registered churches. According to the following report, study conducted by the Center for the Study of Global Christianity, published in June 2013, China has a higher conversion rate than any other nation in the world:

COUNTRY	CONTINENT	CHRISTIAN AAGR	POPULATION AAGR	NET CHRISTIAN AAGR (CONVERSION)
China	Asia	10.86	1.07	9.79

What does this say? Researchers are predicting that "if the high growth rate continues, China will become the country with the most Christians by 2030."[24]

STRENGTH AND GROWTH IN SOUTH KOREA[25]

South Korea has 29 percent Christians and 23 percent Buddhists, with 46 percent lacking any religious affiliation. However, in 1900, only 1 percent of the country's population was Christian. Since then, the Christian population has consistently grown. Whereas in many parts of the world, Christianity spreads largely among the poor, in South Korea that is not the case. Christianity has begun 293 schools and 46 universities. "Protestants have been widely seen by Korea as the religion of the middle class."[26] With over 20,000 churches, Presbyterianism is the biggest denomination.[27]

The largest church in the world is the Yoido Full Gospel Church on Yeouido Island in central Seoul. It boasted a membership of 760,000 people in 2011 when Pastor Yonggi Cho retired. Also, some claim Seoul, South Korea, has the largest Baptist, Presbyterian, and Methodist churches in the world.[28]

FROM GUTENBERG TO GOOGLE

The world is transitioning out of the Gutenberg world into a Google world. The Gutenberg world was introduced when Johannes Gutenberg invented moveable type, which was the driving force of the Protestant Reformation, begun in 1517. Not only was the Word of God quickly and abundantly available, but literature supporting the Reformation was also accessible.

Moveable type represented letters and words that could be formed, changed, and constantly employed to communicate Christianity to the world. As a result, the Gutenberg world produced vast cultures of people who read, wrote, interpreted, and understood the Scriptures. To read, people thought lineally; they placed their ideas that were represented by word symbols into sequence. Together, these words became sentences. Ideas were linked together to give meaning and understanding, which led to thinking rationally in sequence, enabling conclusions to be drawn. As a result, Gutenberg produced a world that was rational and logical. So, Western Christianity communicates the message of Christianity in a rational and logical presentation.

But the world no longer thinks only like Gutenberg. Today's world is driven by Google. Google is one of the world's largest sources of information, including almost all facts and data. The Google world is EPIC: experiential, participatory, image-rich, and connective. This means people interface with the world through EPIC data streams. Therefore, people in the modern world want to experience data rather than just think rationally and logically about it. Data become meaningful to them when they experience it, not necessarily when they understand it.

How can a church interact with the world today? It can do so by becoming more experiential rather than limiting communication to intellectual and logical thought. A logical Bible study of Matthew will not be as effective as a person experiencing Jesus and knowing Him personally. The same applies to worship. They don't want to sing ideas that are logical and practical. They want to experience worship and sing praises to their heavenly Father. This does not rule out logic; rationality still is important. But people have a greater goal; they live in a taste-and-see world.

RELATIONSHIP EVANGELISM LEADS TO GROWTH

Western Christianity presents Christianity in words and doctrine. It also depends on persuasion evangelism, confrontational evangelism, and/or advertising evangelism. However, the expansion of the Global South church rides on the wings of communicating Jesus in relationships. Isn't Christianity all about Jesus? Maybe people will relate to

Jesus and His message through relationships better than through rational understanding of the four spiritual laws.

Remember Jesus invited people, saying, *"Follow Me..."* (Matt. 4:19). Shouldn't that be the way people are invited into a church fellowship? Isn't Jesus the church? Aren't the unsaved to follow Him?

Again, remember that doctrine divides, while the Person of Jesus attracts or draws people to Himself. Therefore, when Christianity is focused in a person, that is, Jesus, it is an attractional movement. The Global South church is introducing people to Jesus Christ by a living relationship (cells, house churches, family evangelism, etc.).

And what does this do? It helps heal the brokenness of humans today. People's relationship with God is broken. Many suffer broken relationships with others. And many have a broken relationship with themselves. They eat themselves into poor health, smoke themselves to an early grave, or destroy themselves with drugs, alcohol, or other self-indulgent wounds. But Jesus restores relationships (with themselves and with others) and gives healing and wholeness.

INCARNATIONAL MINISTRY

Remember Jesus commanded us to go and *"...make disciples of all the nations or cultures"* (Matt. 28:19 ELT). We are to make individual disciples in each and every nation. But He also said to *"make disciples of all...cultures,"* which suggests we are to influence our cultures, or "Christianize" them. The church must live in a culture, bring people to know Jesus Christ in that culture, and then make that culture like Jesus.

This suggests an incarnational ministry. Jesus is introduced into the life of unsaved family and friends; they become part of a church, which is Jesus; and then Jesus is introduced into the culture. Just as the Son of God was incarnated into a human body in the virgin birth,

t be incarnational in churches, for the church is His body.
l ministry is not just rational preaching of Christianity in
ie Gospel is a Person; it is Jesus. So, the Gospel seed that
ited in the hearts of others is the Person of Jesus Christ.

And don't forget that when a seed is planted in soil, the plant and fruit that come from the seed take on the taste of the soil while also retaining the taste of the original seed. Therefore, churches will look like the culture in which they are planted while at the same time looking like Jesus in that culture.

Christianity is unique because it is the only religion where truth is a Person (incarnational).

Western Christianity has developed a failed attraction, for example, "Come to our church building." No, a church is Jesus, and the unsaved must be invited to come to know Him. Western Christianity has a wrong approach. Rather than "Let me explain to you the nature of salvation that Jesus Christ offers," the approach should be "Let me introduce you to Jesus, who will save you."

And Western Christianity has blindly followed colonialism, expressing the attitude that "all Christians should have our Western culture." No, when Jesus lives in a body of believers, He should look like the people of that culture who have come to know Him and follow Him. Then the church should look like that culture. The ultimate aim is to make the culture of that country look like Jesus.

People need to experience God, not just have rational thoughts about Him. People live in a *karaoke* culture; they want to interact and connect with others, their ideas, and their futures. People don't want to just listen to messages so they can hear and understand the Bible. They want to experience God's Word.

The church must shift from a performance presentation where message is delivered to them. Nowadays, people want to participate in the Gospel.

Whereas Gutenberg communicated by word symbols, now people communicate by images, actions, and stories. Today's culture is picture rich and image driven.

Have you noticed that the advertising industry utilizes stories told within a 10- or 30-second commercial? Television captures the imagination, stokes desires, and fulfills dreams. All of this is experienced immediately. Jesus must be presented in the same way.

Commercialization has done something else. It has produced a culture of individualization. Each person is considered an important individual within his/her culture, even though he/she lives, thinks, and breathes in relationships with others. Therefore, the Gospel must connect people to a relationship that connects them to Jesus. No longer can the preacher just tell people the truth or explain the facts of the Bible or make a rational explanation of Christianity. People must relate to Christianity by relating to a believer who communicates Jesus to them. This explains the attraction of home cells, or house churches. These churches are effective. Christians in house churches relate to their friends, families, and neighbors. Within that connective relationship, the unsaved family and friends are walked to Jesus Christ.

Notice how social media is causing a shift to a connectional society. As a result, today's world focuses on community—global community. Isn't that the nature of Christianity, that is, a community of believers?

So what does that mean? It means that Global South churches are reaching people easier through relationships, connection, participation, and community.

WHAT MUST WE DO?

'ore and make disciples of all the nations [help people learn of , and live like Me], baptizing them in the name of the Father and of the Son and of the Holy Spirit so they identify with other followers ["congregationalize" them] *teaching them to observe everything that I have commanded you; and lo, I am with you always [I will indwell you, live in your church and empower you], even to the end of the age"* (Matt. 28:19-20 AMP).

- Missional component—"Go."

- Directional component—make disciples, followers.

- Influential component—influence all cultures with Jesus.

- Salvational component—all people can have a relationship with Jesus.

- Relational component—God planned believers to assemble (church) with other believers to worship Jesus, learn, serve, and fellowship with Jesus and one another.

- Multiplying component—once you plant a church, it must purpose to plant another church just like it.

- Omega component—multiplying reproducing churches is the formula to reach all cultures so that Jesus Christ can return (see Matt. 24:14).

CHAPTER 3

PLANTING REPRODUCING CHURCHES BY CELLS

One of the most unique church planting stories in Christianity is the beginning and growth of the Full Gospel Church on Yeouido Island, South Korea. To understand what God is doing in the world today, it is necessary to understand how Pastor Yonggi Cho laid a biblical foundation to build the largest local church in history.

The path to unlimited church potential is found in the division of small cells within a church. Cho calls these "home cells." They are not the same as a house church. Each home cell is the extension of one mother church into the life of the small group. On the other hand, a house church is usually independent of a large mother church or other house churches. So this is not a story of planting house churches but using home cells to reach into every part of a mother church geographically, culturally, socioeconomically, and racially.

49

Cho learned "pretty good" English as he ran errands for US soldiers who served in the Signal Corps during the Korean conflict.

As a young boy, he rejected the life of disease and poverty and planned to become a medical doctor. However, he contracted tuberculosis, and his doctors gave him no hope of living. The unanswered prayers of Buddhists did not heal him. Cho invited Jesus Christ into his life, and as a result, he was saved, healed, and began following Him.

Following his graduation from the Full Gospel Bible Institute in Seoul in 1958, he planned to go to the United States to study for ministry. However, a woman who would become his future mother-in-law invited him to help her plant and organize a church in her home.

Cho knew very little about how to start a church. He went door to door inviting people to the meeting. Then he went to the top of a hill, yelling at the top of his voice inviting people to come to the church meeting. The church outgrew the small home. The United States Army Signal Corps provided a tent to expand the church into the front yard. Then a second and third tent were added, until it extended into a yard next door. Because the church grew, Cho remained with the young congregation.

Cho began each day at 4:30 A.M. in a prayer service and usually worked past midnight. The young congregation grew.

One Sunday, after attending a dawn prayer meeting, preaching two services, and personally baptizing converts, he collapsed in the baptismal tank. He lay stricken on the church platform with church members crying out to God for his healing.

He later told me that he personally had to get up as an act of faith that he was healed. He walked home enduring the pain of the heart attack. The following Sunday, he repeated the actions and again fell in the baptismal tank with a heart attack. This time he couldn't act as if he were healed, because he really wasn't.

The next six months the Holy Spirit hammered into his mind the idea of "the church in the home." He began to think that the church ought to be located in every home of the church members. He went to the board of elders with plans to divide the city into 62 sections, with each elder leading a section. They would do the ministries of a local church in their part of the city.

Some of the elders told him, "No, you must resign and let us get someone who can lead the church." The elders reiterated that it was not their duty to pastor home churches; they felt it was his duty to pastor these home groups.

Later, his mother-in-law told him, "The women will do it." He assigned various women to lead the 62 house churches. They began meeting to carry out ministry in each house cell.

Cho told his cell leaders, "As Christ is dependent on me, I am a coworker with the Lord. In this new plan, you are coworkers with the Lord of the harvest." Many of the women wept at these words, responding, "No one has ever treated us with this respect."

By 1964, 85 home groups were in full operation. The church had grown to 3,857 and increased by nearly 1,000 more people after Cho had his original heart attack.

I met with Pastor Cho on August 21, 1978, my twenty-fifth wedding anniversary. My wife, Ruth, waited for me in the main auditorium while I interviewed Cho from 5:00 to 6:00 P.M. that evening in his office.

Cho wanted to let me know that he didn't follow American church growth techniques. He explained, "I could not have built the largest church in the world if I followed the methods of Baptists in the United States."[1]

I immediately wanted to debate him and talk about all the great churches that Baptists had built in the United States, but he continued: "Baptists build their churches through their Sunday school teachers and Sunday school classes." Cho understood better than most that the dynamics of Baptist church growth was dedicated laymen. He continued, "Baptists have to construct a small classroom for every class, and they only use it for one hour a week."[2]

Then Cho made a startling statement: "If I were to grow my church the way Baptists grow, I would have to build a church campus as large as UCLA in Los Angeles, California." Then he asked me a question: "How large is UCLA's campus?"

I had been to the campus and said it was about 12 blocks by 15 blocks. I said it contained many three-story buildings, and some buildings were seven or eight stories high. There were hundreds of buildings.

"Yes...yes," Cho smiled as I gave my answer. "That university is as large as my church. I have 100,000 people in my church today, and I would have to build a church campus 15 blocks by 12 blocks if I were to follow the Baptist model." Then Cho went on to explain that he didn't have the money to build a complex that vast, nor would the city of Seoul, South Korea, allow him to do so. "So," he explained, "I use living rooms in homes, laundry rooms, and exercise rooms in apartment buildings to build my church...and I don't have to pay for them."[3]

Cho said that he had 15,358 cell groups that met each week throughout the whole city of Seoul. "These cell groups produce spiritual energy that grows our church. In these small groups, people worship together, study the Word of God, pray, and fellowship, and from these groups, they reach out to win other people to Jesus Christ."

Then Cho asked me a penetrating question: "What is the best picture or analogy of the church in the Bible?"

I answered, "The body...the Body of Christ."

"Exactly," Cho replied. "The body is made up of cells—thousands and millions of cells. My church is one body made up of thousands of cells, and one day I hope to have one million people in cells."

Cho explained that a cell in a human body begins when the semen of a man joins the egg of a woman. All the life of that man and that woman is found in that first cell. In the same way, he explained, all the life of his church was found in the people who made up his cell groups. Then he said, "The secret of the growth of the church is found in the cell; the body grows by the division of cells."[4]

Then Cho asked me, "What happens if a cell in the body grows?" I was embarrassed at the time and didn't know how to answer. So he quickly added, "A growing cell is cancer that leads to death." Then he explained that the healthy cell divides to make two cells. You cannot tell which cell was the original. Hence the secret of the largest church in the world: *the church body grows by the division of home cells.*[5]

Cho explained that when a home cell averages over 15 in attendance, it is divided into two cells, then each cell will grow.[6]

Wikipedia states that "cell division allows for continual construction and reproduction...an entire new organism is created."[7] It also suggests that the human body experiences ten quadrillion cell divisions in a lifetime. The division occurs, and genetic information (DNA) is stored and must be replicated.[8]

Just as the secret of physical growth is healthy cells, the secret of church growth is healthy home cells. When each home cell does everything that a local church does, then it is healthy and the church will grow and multiply.

All that the body will ultimately become is transferred by DNA and reproduced in each new cell. The life of the mother church determines what the new home cell will become and how it will function. Therefore, the people who plant a new church will determine what it will become. Their *vision* and *values* will hold the new church together.

Genetics has suggested that less than 50 percent of the traits of one cell, sperm, or egg will transfer into the new cell. Sometimes that percentage is often less than 50 percent. Therefore, much—but not all—of the character and nature of a founding church will be seen in the new church as it is established.

Why are some cells cancerous? Sometimes the new cell is not completely committed to the original *vision* from the mother church, nor does it completely buy into the *values* of the mother church. Usually, the closer the new cell is to the power and nature of the original cell, the more strength it has to cause growth, which gives strength back to the mother church. When a church body—or cell—becomes sick or stops growing, it's probably because the new cell drifts away from the *vision* and *values* of the mother church.

Approximately 50 to 70 billion cells die in the human body each day. A small child will have 20 to 30 billion cells die each day. Each cell lives approximately 100 to 120 days before dying.[9] Technically, this means that approximately 1 percent of all the cells in the body will die each day and must be replaced with new growing cells. That says something about creating new home cells or Bible classes to keep a local church growing. It also indicates that some older or existing cells will necessarily die.

That means it's alright for a church or group/cell within a church to die and/or be eliminated. Why? Because a new church or cell will take its place. New healthy cell groups produce a new healthy church. A church's health is not necessarily dependent on the continuation of all groups. So, the church leaders should expect the death of some church cells and never feel surprised or a sense of failure when it happens.

What controls the division of cells within the physical body? When a cell has an error in its DNA so that it cannot be repaired and/or replicated, that cell will die. That means the healthy body will get rid of old cells that it doesn't need or can't use. Then existing cells will break apart to form a future healthy body. Old cells are recycled into and through the white blood cells and eventually out of the body.

Therefore, the health of the overall church is determined by the health of each cell. Or a total church is as healthy as each cell group. That means God must regulate each cell if it is to remain healthy.

We learn from genetics that if errors in the cell and/or a church group are not repaired, it will die. That's another way of saying that cells in church must be committed to the original DNA of the body (its vision and values), or it will be recycled and die. Churches die because people may drift into another ministry or another church and also because they are not properly recycled and divided.

What is cancer? Cancer is the result of the disruption of the division of cells so that the cell continues to produce more unhealthy cells. Have you ever seen a church produce unhealthy cells by doing things that do not contribute to its growth?

When people in a cell or church group proceed without any order, or rule of ministry, they will deform the body. That can lead to a church's death. What people do in small groups by studying, praying, fellowshipping, and interacting with one another determines the health of the cell, which determines the health of the body/church as a whole.

In my first meeting with Pastor Cho, he explained what would destroy a local cell group or church:

1. *Time constraints.* Cho said that some immature leaders get excited about the Holy Spirit and the Bible lesson of the day and lead the meeting for three or four hours. That will often kill a cell. Because most members are conscientious and will remain for three or four hours, the next day they may fall asleep at work or they may struggle to keep up with the normal

duties of life. They could get fired and/or eventually drop out of the cell. The commitment of cell leaders to time constraints will determine the health and the continual reproduction of the cell.

2. *Doctrinal constraints.* Cho explained that sometimes leaders get excited about new doctrines and teach on and on about them instead of teaching the Bible. Those with little discipline to teach the assigned lesson usually drift into heresy. This ultimately hurts the church and kills the cell. Therefore, he insists that each leader teach the outline he provides. "If they don't," he said, "fire them." He mentioned that they must be replaced for the good of the body, not just because they have disregarded his directions.

3. *Hospitality constraints.* Cho told me that those in a small cell must never serve more than hot tea and a cookie for one person. He mentioned that some ladies want to impress their friends so they serve two, three, or four cookies along with hot tea. Then beyond cookies, it becomes a liver pâté sandwich and ultimately a whole roasted duck. He said money becomes a factor in this cell group, and as a result, competition and greed kills the life of the cell group. So, when people break the rules about serving too much food, "fire them."

STRENGTHS OF CHURCH CELLS

There are obvious strengths in the small-group method as well as some hidden weaknesses. Those who use small groups should understand the following assets.

First, small groups give a doorway into local church membership because people come into a friendly, warm setting in a small group and feel acceptance. Small groups usually attract people like its members because "like attracts like." Therefore, in small groups, the attraction factor eliminates the barriers that keep people out of churches. These barriers can be the church building, the ecclesiastical service, some "dead" members, or negative criticism.

Second, small groups lead to conversion growth in churches because people identify with other people and are attracted to people like themselves in a small group. Barriers are taken down, and someone who understands questions about the church usually answers their questions. Because small groups usually do not meet in the church building but rather out in the community, the ministry is able to reach people where they are and make them feel welcome.

Third, small groups assimilate new members into local churches. People take the first step toward church membership by becoming part of a group. When they find church barriers removed, they become open to church membership, which may involve baptism and other requirements.

Small groups usually lead to leadership multiplication. When more than one person leads a Bible study or prayer in a small group, they are being prepared to become a leader of their own group. When groups are divided and/or new groups started, people who have been mentored become leaders in the new group.

A fourth strength is in communication of Christian attitudes and core values. In a larger congregational setting, people receive Bible content through teaching, exhortation, and/or explanation; and while they may learn Bible content and/or doctrine through these methods, they sometimes miss the "inner" values of the Christian life. However, in small groups, those values are highlighted as the members pray and testify. They also prize those actions and attitudes, which is a first step toward living as a member of the group. Thus, small groups communicate the "spiritual" aspect of Christianity, not just the rational and/or conceptual aspects of the faith.[10]

	1982	1980	1975	1970	1960
Church Membership	230,000	133,000	22,992	8,252	800
Weekly Cell Groups	15,358	9,000	755	167	76
New Members Per Day	133	60	8	2	2

*Based on the above data, the church experienced an explosive growth rate of 1,512 percent from 1970 to 1980.[11]

Cho retired in 2010 with an estimated 760,000 worshipers in attendance. This represented approximately 50 satellite churches (multisites) and 34,000 home cell groups. I preached at the 7:00 A.M. early service in 2011. He preached at the 8:00 A.M. service. He told me that half of the cell groups and all 50 satellite churches were released to become independent or indigenous churches in 2010. Approximately 300,000 worshipers were in attendance at the mother church at that time.

Many people have doubted the statistical numbers as reported by the church. I have found that the home groups were so attractive to friends, families, and neighbors that many from other churches, including Presbyterian and Baptist churches, have become involved in Cho's home cells, ultimately swelling the attendance far beyond any human expectations. That means that many of the attendees in home groups are church members of other mainline churches, not Cho's church. Therefore, his figure of 760,000 is probably a correct figure, and those who doubted that figure were also accurate. An understanding of the Korean culture and how they embrace and relate to family and friends will help understand the differences in the count.

CHAPTER 4

THE BIBLICAL MANDATE FOR PLANTING REPRODUCING CHURCHES

Jesus introduced the idea of the church to the disciples by saying, "*... upon this rock I will build my church, and all the powers of hell will not conquer it*" (Matt. 16:18 NLT). There are two forces in this promise. First, there is an omnipotent force of Jesus Christ, who will build His assembly or *ecclesia*, that is, the church. The second force is hell and evil that opposes, but will not conquer, the church.

CHALLENGE

From this prophecy, we see an eternal conflict between good and evil, between God and satan, both attempting to conquer and defeat the other. But the promise of Jesus Christ is that "He will be victorious." And what is the victory? It is the salvation of eternal souls born in sin, ruled by their evil nature, and captured by satan. The outward sign of victory is when they identify with the church of Jesus Christ. The other component to this victory—ultimately satan will be destroyed and evil done away with.

God's victory in this eternal conflict with satan is seen in the strategy Jesus gave called the "Great Commission." His command can be summarized in the following way: *"Go and preach the Gospel of salvation to every person in the world, winning them to salvation, baptizing them into a local assembly of believers, teaching them to obey everything that He has taught while on earth, and that local assembly will struggle victoriously against evil and will continue the battle by planting other churches that will do the same task that it does"* (see Mark 16:15).

The Great Commission not only targets every individual in the world; it also targets every culture. Jesus explained, *"Go and make disciples of all the nations (ethne, people groups)"* (Matt. 28:19 ELT). When Jesus included the nations, He was suggesting that a local assembly of His believers would be planted in every culture or tribe within the world as a witness to everyone in that tribe, with the view of winning everyone in that tribe to Jesus Christ (see Matt. 24:14).

But why have so many foreign mission endeavors been fruitless? I didn't say they have been wrong. Any time we obey Jesus Christ, we have served God well. But some foreign missions have not been as productive and/or fruitful as they could have been. Let's not blame our failure or weak results on satan and his evil influence. Let's look first to the work of the church. Could it have been more effective or successful?

Perhaps our foreign missions effort has been fruitless because some of their work has not included church planting. All evangelism has its place: radio evangelism, television evangelism, medical evangelism, mass evangelism, personal evangelism, education and humanitarian evangelism, etc. Saturation evangelism, or using every available means to reach every available person at every available time, is still a dominant strategy.[1] However, God's primary method of evangelizing the nations of the world is planting a New Testament church to reach individuals and to influence the culture in which lost people are located. And since multiplication is God's plan beginning at creation, then God's plan for the church is to multiply by planting reproducing churches.

THE MANDATE OF THE GREAT COMMISSION

The Great Commission was given at five different times in separate locations. Why was this important command reiterated over a period of 40 days in various locations? Why didn't Jesus just give the entire Great Commission all at once?

Perhaps there was a lack of learning readiness by the disciples. Remember, they were spiritually blinded and did not expect the cross and truly did not expect the resurrection. They had tunnel vision about the Old Testament. During those 40 days, the Holy Spirit illuminated their minds (removed their blindness) so that they could more completely understand the prophecies in the Old Testament about the Messiah's death, burial, and resurrection.

Also, during those 40 days they harmonized the truth of the Old Testament with the facts of Jesus' life and death. When they began following Jesus, they probably had a very limited view of the atonement. Later, through the ministry of Paul's teaching on justification, they were able to more fully understand that through salvation a person was declared righteous and fully accepted by God because they were placed in Christ Jesus.

There was another reason why the Great Commission was given five times. Jesus' followers were Jews, and their minds were culturally closed to God's plan to evangelize all Gentiles, everyone in the world.

During the 40 days, they were filled with the Holy Spirit so they learned and understood the Scriptures in a clear light (see John 20:22-23). Also, the Holy Spirit's indwelling developed their faith to receive the new commission and act upon it.

Why did it take 40 days? It is hard to think outside the box when you have never been outside the box. These first disciples probably did not even know that God was interested in anything outside the Jewish box. And because these disciples had lived within the Jewish culture, they rejected Gentile culture. A good Jew had nothing to do with the culture of the Gentiles around them (see Acts 10:45-46).

THE FIRST GIVING OF THE GREAT COMMISSION
JOHN 20:19-21

That Sunday evening the disciples were meeting behind locked doors because they were afraid of the Jewish leaders. Suddenly, Jesus was standing there among them! "Peace be with you," He said. As He spoke, He showed them the wounds in His hands and His side. They were filled with joy when they saw the Lord! Again He said, "Peace be with you. As the Father has sent Me, so I am sending you" (John 20:19-21 NLT).

This was Easter Sunday afternoon, and ten of them were assembled together. They were fearful of the Jews because the authorities had crucified their Lord. Fear of death does strange things to people, and so it is not strange that these disciples were huddled together out of fear.

They gathered in the Upper Room again, the same room where they celebrated the first communion service with Jesus. The doors were locked. This was a Dutch door. The Upper Room had been used for banquets; the upper door was open for serving food, and the lower part of the door was closed to keep out animals. Both doors were locked against intruders. Also, Jesus couldn't get into the room. Then Jesus materialized before them and showed them His hands and side (see John 20:20). This is the proof of His death. When they saw—*eidw* (not merely looking, but the Greek word suggests touching and handling)—they were convinced that this was the same Jesus that had died.

"Peace be with you" was the first thing that Jesus said to them in the Upper Room, reminding them of the last words He gave to them in that same Upper Room: *"...in Me you may have peace. In the world you will have tribulation..."* (John 20:20 NLT; John 16:33 ESV). He fulfilled His last prediction with His presence. This should have encouraged them to believe the next things He would say to them.

"As the Father has sent me, so I am sending you" (John 20:21 NLT). The key word here is *Father.* Remember, Jesus' use of the personal word *Father* was one of the key words used in John, appearing over 150 times. Just as the Father sent Jesus alone into the world, now Jesus is sending the apostles; but He will be their escort. The word *send* (*apostelloie*) tells them they have a message to send and a mission to accomplish.

But notice that His command did not tell them where to go, to whom to speak, what to do, or even how to get the job done. His first command was simply a command to *go.* Where should they go? Were they ready to go?

It is not evident whether the disciples were confused or ready to obey. Remember, in that day, Jews were scattered around the world in what is called the "dispersion." Did the disciples think they were being sent to the Jews in dispersion? Perhaps none of them in the room fully understood that the message included Gentiles—all Gentiles.

"He breathed on them...the Holy Spirit" (John 20:22 NLT). Just as God breathed into Adam's nostrils the breath of life, so Jesus breathed

the Holy Spirit into them. What was this? It was probably not the breath of salvation—they gained that when they obeyed and followed Jesus originally. Perhaps this was a temporary Old Testament filling, the same filling experienced by Moses, many of the judges, and David. They would be filled with the Holy Spirit until they were permanently baptized with the Holy Spirit on the Day of Pentecost.

"If you forgive anyone's sins, they are forgiven…" (John 20:23 NLT). Notice their sins would not be forgiven by a church authority, nor did they need the authority of the priest in the temple or even the high priest. Jesus bypassed the entire sacrificial system of the temple when He gave the authority of salvation. Now, everything had changed. They probably didn't understand what He meant until later. One of their tasks was to tell everyone that salvation was now centered in Jesus Christ. It was all made possible by His death, burial, and resurrection.

The text does not tell us how Jesus left them. We cannot believe that He opened the locked doors and walked out, leaving them inside. The text does not tell how long He stayed. All the text gives us is the essence of what happened that evening. That included everything Jesus said to them that was important. Probably Jesus left as He entered: He suddenly disappeared.

What happened that Sunday through the following Saturday is unknown. We can image certain things occurred. First, they would have prayed much to God the Father. They would have begun studying carefully the Old Testament Scriptures concerning the Messiah. They would have discussed among themselves all the words that Jesus taught them while He was with them. They would have tried to analyze and apply everything that Jesus had told them to do. Obviously, it was a life-changing week.

THE SECOND GIVING OF THE GREAT COMMISSION
MARK 16:14-16; JOHN 20:24-29

Eight days later the disciples were together again, and this time Thomas was with them. The doors were locked; but suddenly, as before, Jesus was standing among them. "Peace be with you," He said. Then He said to Thomas, "Put your finger here, and look at My hands. Put your hand into the wound in My side. Don't be faithless any longer. Believe!" (John 20:26-28 NLT)

A week earlier, there were ten disciples in the Upper Room when they met Jesus on Easter Sunday afternoon. Judas had hung himself. For some reason that we do not know, Thomas had gone and hidden himself. Remember, Thomas is called the "doubter." He likely doubted his doubts and perhaps ran away further and hid deeper than the other disciples. But a week later he joined them.

They were together in the same Upper Room; perhaps this place was becoming more comfortable to them. Or perhaps that is where they had the Last Supper with Jesus, or it was the place where He last appeared to them.

One of the twelve disciples, Thomas (nicknamed the Twin), was not with the others when Jesus came. They told him, "We have seen the Lord!" (John 20:24 NLT)

Jesus had established His credibility when He allowed them to see and touch His wounds. They had seen—*oraw* (to perceive and analyze carefully) (see John 20:20).

Thomas is an example to all of us who are fearful, unbelieving, and just can't accept facts. Thomas had said, *"...I will not believe"* (John 20:25). So, he signifies the others in the Christian tradition who will have the same unbelief. Jesus invited Thomas to do what the other ten disciples had probably done the previous week—touch His wounds.

Jesus gave the divine paradox, *"...Don't be faithless any longer. Believe!"* (John 20:27 NLT).

Did Thomas put his fingers into the hand wounds of Jesus? Did he thrust his fist into His side wound? The Bible does not say. But he cried out a great statement of faith: *"My Lord and my God!"* (John 20:28 NLT). This is perhaps the strongest expression of deity for Jesus Christ found in Scripture. Jesus is the LORD; that is, He is Jehovah of the Old Testament, the "I Am that I Am" of eternity. But Jesus is also God, the Elohim Creator of Genesis chapter 1. Thomas's statement came from the illumination of the Holy Spirit.

Mark describes the events in the Upper Room that evening but leaves out the story of Thomas:

> *Still later He appeared to the eleven disciples as they were eating together. He rebuked them for their stubborn unbelief because they refused to believe those who had seen Him after He had been raised from the dead. And then He told them, "Go into all the world and preach the Good News to everyone. Anyone who believes and is baptized will be saved. But anyone who refuses to believe will be condemned"* (Mark 16:14-16 NLT).

If the other disciples had any questions—what they must do, what they must preach, where they must preach, etc.—Jesus answered those questions in this second Lord's Day appearance. He commands, *"Go into all the world and preach the Good News to everyone"* (Mark 16:15 NLT).

Now Jesus is giving them a borderless ministry, that is, "go everywhere in the whole world." He is also giving them a limitless ministry, that is, "go to every person in the world (not just the Jews)." Finally, He is giving them an eternal ministry, that is, "anyone who believes will be saved." This was the great promise of salvation. And what is the opposite? Those who refuse to believe will be condemned.

THE THIRD GIVING OF THE GREAT COMMISSION
MATTHEW 28:16-20

Then the eleven disciples left for Galilee, going to the mountain where Jesus had told them to go. When they saw Him, they worshiped Him—but some of them doubted! Jesus came and told His disciples, "I have been given all authority in heaven and on earth. Therefore, go and make disciples of all the nations, baptizing them in the name of the Father and the Son and the Holy Spirit. Teach these new disciples to obey all the commands I have given you. And be sure of this: I am with you always, even to the end of the age" (Matthew 28:16-20 NLT).

Previously, the disciples were gathered together in Jerusalem in the Upper Room, and they had stayed in Jerusalem approximately one week, that is, from Easter Sunday to the following Sunday. Matthew does not give the exact time when Jesus appeared to them in Galilee. We do not know where the mountain is located. This could have been the mountain known today as the Mount of Beatitudes, between Capernaum and Tiberius, or it could be another mountain where the 5,000 were fed. While we do not know where the mountain was located, we know some of the things that took place there.

"...*Some of them doubted*" (Matt. 28:17 NLT). Even though Jesus had appeared to the disciples, some still doubted. Perhaps the 11 disciples did not doubt because they had touched Jesus. The doubters were part of a greater multitude. Paul calls them "about 500 followers" (see 1 Cor. 15:6).

On this occasion, Jesus told them, *"I have been given all authority in heaven and on earth"* (Matt. 28:18 NLT). So, He commanded, *"Therefore, go and make disciples of all the nations..."* (Matt. 28:19 NLT).

There is a world of meaning in each of the words in this command.

"Go" is not an imperative, that is, a command (Matt. 28:19 NLT). Jesus had already commanded in His previous appearances for them to go. This is a participle. Jesus is assuming that they are going. It means "as you are going." A participle implies continuous action, so they must be going continuously into all the world.

"...Make disciples..." (Matt. 28:19 NLT). This command is similar to Jesus' invitation for people to follow Him as disciples. He is now telling His disciples to get others to follow Him. Everything the disciples have done by following Jesus others must now do.

And what is *disciple-making*? It begins by obeying the Lord, then knowing and learning the Lord, next loving the Lord, and finally doing what He commands. Soon Jesus will tell them to baptize converts as evidence of their willingness to follow Him.

Notice disciple-making is more than decision-making. He did not want people to just know about Himself, that is, to know biblical content. He did not want followers to mouth the words, "I believe." He wanted people to follow Him as the disciples had followed Him.

"...Baptizing them in the name of the Father and the Son and the Holy Spirit" (Matt. 28:19 NLT). Just as John the Baptist had come baptizing people in water and calling people to repentance, so now Jesus wants them to baptize people in like manner. John's baptism was looking forward to the coming Messiah, that is, looking to the future. Their baptism would look backward to Jesus' death, burial, and resurrection. Followers would be immersed into water, which is symbolic of dying with Jesus. As Jesus was placed in a grave, a

new believer would be placed in a watery grave symbolically. Therefore, dying with Jesus, their sins would be removed and they would be forgiven.

When a new believer is brought up from their watery grave, it signifies their new life in Jesus Christ, as they are identified with Him in His resurrection. So, the baptismal formula is symbolic of their transformation—their new life received in Jesus Christ. People would not just be outward followers but would be inwardly transformed by the message. They would receive new life to follow Christ.

Baptism was tied to evangelism: not only must people believe in Jesus Christ and begin following Him, they must identify with Him in death, burial, and resurrection. They must "die with Christ" and then go out and "live for Christ." When new converts were baptized in a church fellowship, they were assembling together. Therefore, baptism was more than just personal identification with Christ; it was a symbol of assembling together and/or congregationalizing new believers.

"Teaching them to observe..." (Matt. 28:20). All new believers must go beyond baptism; they must learn everything Jesus taught His disciples. Therefore, the message of the Gospel is not complete until it is taught to every new believer.

"...Make disciples of all the nations..." (Matt. 28:19). The disciples were to target every *ethne*, meaning every people group and/or tribe. This is the culture where the unsaved lived.

Remember, God loves the various cultures of the world, which God created when He changed the language of the people at the Tower of Babel. A new language is more than just verbal symbols of meaning. Words carry meaning, value, and life. Words affirm our living, and words are used to express our life. Therefore, when God changed the language of the people, He changed their culture and their life, ultimately changing the things they valued.

When the Bible says that God rejoices over His people, it means He gets pleasure out of the different expressions of each culture (see Zeph. 3:17). While love is the same in all cultures, people express their love in different ways in different cultures. The same goes for honesty and mercy. Each culture expresses these qualities through their own words and actions. Therefore, God rejoices to see how people in different cultures express genuine love to Him from the integrity of those cultures.

It is hard for people in Western Christianity to realize that God not only loves their Western Christianity, but also loves the African culture, the Scandinavian culture, and the culture of the Aborigines and the Chinese. He loves all cultures equally.

Now Jesus was telling His disciples to take the Gospel to every culture in the world—and not just preach to them, but also make disciples of them. That disciple-making process would end up building a congregation to influence each culture so that Christ is expressed there.

Therefore, the enculturation of Jesus Christ is best done by church planting. Remember, personal evangelism is not enough, nor are the other forms of evangelism enough to carry out the heart of God. It will take a church being planted in a new culture to influence that culture for the glory of God.

THE FOURTH GIVING OF THE GREAT COMMISSION
LUKE 24:46-50

What was Jesus teaching during the 40 days? Luke gives an account of the content of His teaching when Jesus explained the credibility of the new message: *"...all things must be fulfilled..."* (Luke 24:44). He is saying that the predictions of His death, burial, and resurrection in the Old Testament were fulfilled at Calvary. Jesus taught them the entire Old Testament when He included *"...in the law of Moses and the Prophets and the Psalms..."* (Luke 24:44). The reference to Moses was a reference to the first five books of the Old Testament written by Moses. These five books were usually kept in one scroll. The second scroll included the major prophet books: Isaiah, Jeremiah, Lamentations, Ezekiel, and Daniel. The third scroll began with the Psalms. When Jesus referred to the Psalms, He included the historical, poetical books, as well as the minor prophets. So, Jesus gave them a survey of the entire Old Testament concerning Himself, including references to Himself in predictions, types, and symbols. Then Jesus explains:

> *Yes, it was written long ago that the Messiah would suffer and die and rise from the dead on the third day. It was also written that this message would be proclaimed in the authority of His name to all the nations, beginning in Jerusalem: "There is forgiveness of sins for all who repent." You are witnesses of all these things. And now I will send the Holy Spirit, just as My Father promised. But stay here in the city until the Holy Spirit comes and fills you with power from heaven* (Luke 24:46-50 NLT).

And what was the new message they were to preach? *"...That the Messiah would suffer and die and rise from the dead on the third day"* (Luke 24:46 NLT). It was the vicarious substitutionary atonement, so the death of Christ was sufficient for all the world (Jews and Gentiles) and efficient for the salvation of all who believed. The Jewish temple sacrifices were no longer efficacious.

And what did this message include? *"There is forgiveness of sins for all who repent"* (Luke 24:47 NLT). No longer would they have to go to the temple to sacrifice a lamb, because Jesus was the Lamb who died for them (see John 1:29). They no longer had to go through the temple sacrifices; they could go directly to God through Jesus Christ. And what do they get? *Forgiveness!*

So, what was their task? *"You are witnesses of all these things"* (Luke 24:48 NLT). A witness is one who shares the experience of what he/she has seen, heard, and felt. Therefore, not only would they tell the world about the message of the death, burial, and resurrection, but they had to share their personal salvation experience, that is, what they knew and felt and how they responded to the message from God. They were to be witnesses.

Then Jesus gave them a third task: *"...stay here in the city until the Holy Spirit comes and fills you with power from heaven"* (Luke 24:49 NLT). The King James Version uses the word *tarry.* They would be waiting and praying until the Holy Spirit came upon them. The disciples probably did not know how long they were to wait, but the Holy Spirit would come on the Day of Pentecost.

However, Jesus led the 11 disciples out of the city of Jerusalem and began walking toward the Mount of Olives. He was in His resurrected body; the disciples saw Him, talked with Him, and listened to Him. Did others see Him? That we do not know.

THE FIFTH GIVING OF THE GREAT COMMISSION
ACTS 1:6-9

It was likely only a few hours after the fourth giving of the Great Commission that they arrived at the Mount of Olives on the east side of the city.

The disciples continually asked Jesus, *"Lord, has the time come for You to free Israel and restore our kingdom?"* (Acts 1:6 NLT). They were still looking for the Kingdom of God that was promised to David and the Old Testament saints. Perhaps the disciples thought that all their trials and tribulations would be wrapped up and God's Kingdom would come to earth then and there.

Perhaps they were thinking of rewards and what they would get from serving Jesus Christ. But God's calendar is different than man's. Jesus answered, *"The Father alone has the authority to set those dates and times, and they are not for you to know"* (Acts 1:7 NLT).

How often we forget that last exhortation of Jesus: *"...not for you to know"* (Acts 1:7 NLT). Most want to know when Christ will come and what will happen in the future. But we should remember that it is not for us to know. Our duty is to obey Him, love one another, and fulfill His commission.

Jesus did not give them another command to go evangelize the world; He had already done that. But He tells them what will happen after they receive the Holy Spirit. Remember, He has already commanded them to wait and pray in Jerusalem for the Holy Spirit. Now He says:

> *"But you will receive power when the Holy Spirit comes upon you. And you will be My witnesses, telling people about Me everywhere—in Jerusalem, throughout Judea, in Samaria, and to the ends of the earth." After saying this, He was taken up into a cloud while they were watching, and they could no longer see Him* (Acts 1:8-9 NLT).

"You will receive power..." (Acts 1:8 NLT). Do you think the disciples understood what that power meant? Did they know how to use it? Do you think that they understood that power included physical miracles? Do you think they understood the power that a church would have over a culture? Did they know what the influence of the Gospel would have over an entire nation?

The fifth giving of the Great Commission deals with *geography*. Jesus had assumed they would go, so now He gives a geographical strategy to carry out the Great Commission.

Jerusalem. That is their home environment. They were to begin preaching Jesus where they lived. Every person is to evangelize their "Jerusalem," which is their home environment. They must do the same as the early disciples did. Notice the accusations of the world against the church: *"...you have filled all Jerusalem with your teaching about Him..."* (Acts 5:28 NLT).

Judea. The Greek language connects *kai de* with Jerusalem, meaning, "Both Jerusalem and all of Judea at the same time." When we evangelize our whole area of Jerusalem, we must also evangelize the surrounding area. It may be the outskirts of our metropolitan area, or the county, or other connecting geographical area. A Gospel witness should never be limited to a locality but should permeate every area where people are living.

Samaria. The Samaritans would be different from the people living in Jerusalem. It would be a different culture, and Jesus has already told them about taking the Gospel into all cultures. Samaria means cross-cultural evangelism, or one culture, for example, Western culture, carrying the Gospel to people of another culture, for example, Hispanic culture. But in the process of cross-cultural evangelism, the church should be planted in the new culture so that every local church will follow through with "in-culture evangelism." Therefore, all cross-cultural evangelism should lead to in-culture evangelism.

"...To the ends of the earth" (Acts 1:8 NLT). Here Jesus does not focus on every culture, but He is talking about every place in the world. He wants us to cover all areas geographically with the Gospel.

Witness. Again, Jesus uses the term *witness*. A witness is one who shares what he/she has experienced, felt, and seen. This experience must be communicated to everyone else. Therefore, the church shouldn't depend on secular methods to preach the Gospel. It may use secular media—for example, radio, television, newspapers—or any other form to get the Gospel out. But the church must go and witness the Gospel to every person.

Remember, when Jesus gave the Great Commission in Matthew 28, the focus was on results. They were to get disciples in every nation. But in this last giving, the emphasis is on geography—sharing the Gospel with every person, everywhere, at all times. It is a geographical command.

By illustration, New Testament Christians did as Jesus commanded; they went everywhere establishing New Testament churches. As we read carefully the Book of Acts, we do not find any "lone wolf" Christians. They were always associated with other believers, and they were associated together as a testimony to the place where they were located.

The Book of Acts tells the story of disciples going everywhere, successfully planting churches that then planted other churches. As believers were scattered, sometimes by persecution, so the seed of the Gospel took root in various national soils, and in each culture the church began to grow and reach others within that culture.

We see in Acts 9:31 a geographical broadening of the Gospel. Both believers and churches were multiplied *"throughout all Judea, Galilee, and Samaria"* (Acts 9:31). And then the dynamitic church planting efforts by the Apostle Paul, Barnabas, Silas, Timothy, and all the other early disciples demonstrate the concept of planting churches that reproduced themselves.

NOT INCLUDED IN THE GREAT COMMISSION

The command by Jesus is called the "Great Commission." It was given on five different occasions with a different emphasis each time.

The above discussion has analyzed what believers must do in obeying this command. But going further, let's analyze what the Great Commission does not include.

1. *The Great Commission tells us to "go," but it does not tell us how to go.* It does not tell how to mobilize. It does not tell us to get the job done by denominations, mission agencies, individuals, or even how a church should mobilize itself to get the job done.

God has given believers a clear picture of what He expects them to do, but He has not told them how they will carry out the command, what methods will they use, and how will they organize themselves. God and His people are in this task together. They must find the answers together. God's great wisdom and intelligence define our task: "Go!" (see Matt. 28:19). But believers have a responsibility to work out the details. *"We are both God's workers..."* (1 Cor. 3:9 NLT). Elsewhere Paul writes that we are *"God's partners"* (2 Cor. 6:1 NLT).

The Great Commission has a *division of labor*. This is a principle of God and people working together to accomplish His work. God has His task, and we can't do it. We have our task, and God won't do it. Christ's task was to die for the sins of the world; our task is to tell everyone. God's task is to fill or empower us; our task is to use His authority. God's task is to give us the message to preach; our task is to speak it. God's task is to lead us; our task is to follow and work out the details. *"We make our own plans, but God guides our every step"* (see Prov. 16:9).

Therefore, the Great Commission is a partnership between God and believers. God has done His part; now believers must do their part. We must use all our intelligence, all our creativity, and all our strength to carry out the Great Commission.

2. *The Great Commission tells us to preach, but it does not lay out a homiletical guide giving principles of, or practical tips on, preaching.*

Again, in this *division of labor*, humans have a responsibility. God will bless the spoken word, but He has limited Himself to a human's blessability.[2] God will use us according to our usability.

That means humans must develop several abilities at the same time and must perfect each ability as best as they can. The greater number of abilities and the greater mastery of these abilities will result in greater blessings by God.

Humans must expand their vocabulary, expand their voice projection, and expand their emotional persuasion. They must obtain the best education in a wide variety of subjects. The better equipped the believer, the more God can use him/her.

The sharper the pencil, the more accurate it writes.
The more permanent the ink, the longer
the message can be read.
The more intelligent the writer, the more
appropriate the message.
The more yielded to God, the more God uses the messenger.

3. *The Great Commission gives us the Gospel, but it does not give us a complete doctrinal statement. Jesus told us that the Gospel was His death to forgive us our sins, and His resurrection gave us new life that was eternal (see Luke 24:46).* But the Gospel is not a complete doctrinal statement. Perhaps the first was the Apostles' Creed, then the Nicaean Creed. Perhaps the next memorable was the Westminster Confession of Faith. Some might include the New Hampshire Confession of Faith because it was foundational to both the Northern American Baptist Convention and the Southern Baptist Convention.

We must study, struggle to understand, and then apply truth.

Truth is that which is accurate and eternal and is consistent with itself. We search for truth, read it, understand it, interpret it, and then pass it on to the next generation. Divine predestination verses human responsibility was never fully spelled out in Scripture; we must struggle to understand, apply, and obey. The details of doctrine is life's challenge. That is our human quest.

4. *The Great Commission instructs us to use our spiritual gifts to carry out its mandate, but it does not tell us how to use them.* We read, *"When He ascended to the heights, He led a crowd of captives, and gave gifts to His people"* (Eph. 4:8 NLT). All believers were given spiritual gifts (or abilities) at the resurrection. Some were given the spiritual gift of being an apostle, prophet, evangelist, pastor, or teacher (see Eph. 4:11). It does not tell them how to prepare for these tasks, how to perform them, or the attitudes necessary to be successful. Believers are given a spiritual ability, but all must develop their ability to know it, apply it, and convince people. Can we assume that God will give the greatest blessing to those who are best prepared, who best apply their gift, and who are the most faithful?

5. *The Great Commission tells us to make disciples in every culture and to influence cultures for Christ, but it doesn't tell us how to penetrate cultures, how to learn each culture, or how to influence each culture.* This is a challenge to all believers in every culture. Jesus commanded, *"… make disciples of all ethnic groups…"* (Matt. 28:19 ELT). He targeted all of the people groups of the world; none were left out. He did not tell us to start with some cultural groups that are the easiest to penetrate, nor did He tell us which would be the hardest to penetrate. He did not tell us the best cultures. He did tell us He would return when the last cultural group was reached with the Gospel. *"And the Good News about the Kingdom will be preached throughout the whole world, so that all nations will hear it; and then the end will come"* (Matt. 24:14 NLT).

The church has been slow to recognize the mandate to reach cultural groups. This is hard work; it is difficult—almost impossible. It would be an unattainable goal if Jesus didn't promise, *"I will be with you"* and *"you will receive power when the Holy Spirit comes upon you…"* (see Matt. 28:20; Acts 1:8 NLT).

6. *The Great Commission tells us to baptize new believers into the church, but it doesn't tell us how to constitute these churches or how to organize and administer them.* The church is both a divine organism and a human organization. God did His part to institute it, but He left a lot of the organizational and practical implementation to believers. Should churches be led by a pastor, elders, or a bishop? Should churches be governed by an Episcopal polity or representative or congregational model? We are not told how often to meet (there are illustrations of believers meeting each Lord's Day). We are directed to celebrate the Lord's Table *"when ye come together"* (1 Cor. 11:20 KJV). But is that daily, weekly, monthly, quarterly, or annually? In the *division of labor,* much of the formation and administration of the local church is left up to believers as they study and apply Scripture.

7. *The Great Commission tells us to teach all new converts, but it doesn't give us lesson plans or educational tools.* We are given educational outcomes: *"teaching them to observe all things…"* (Matt. 28:20 NKJV). Teaching will not be measured by our methods, techniques, or academic grades. Is God concerned that students make As or a below-average grade? God is concerned with outcomes—"teaching them to obey." The new believer must know more of the Gospel and the content of the Bible. Teaching will be measured by "observe all."

Note that new believers will not be recognized when they learn the introductory aspects of Christianity. *"Let us stop going over the basic teachings about Christ again and again. Let us go on instead and become mature in our understanding…"* (Heb. 6:1 NLT). New believers must go on to maturity in Christ as they obey all Jesus taught.

8. *Obeying the Great Commission is wrapped up in learning languages and cultures, but it does not tell us how to learn languages or cultures or how to use them.* When Jesus instructed the disciples to preach to every person in every culture, He implied that we should use the language of each culture. Jesus suggested that lost people could learn Christ from hearing about Him in their languages and through their languages. On the Day of Pentecost, the Holy Spirit came on all the believers in the Upper Room. There were three signs: first, they heard the roaring of a mighty windstorm; second, flames of fire settled on each of them; and third, they began speaking in other languages (see Acts 2:1-4). They were speaking in other languages, *"as the Holy Spirit gave them this ability"* (Acts 2:4 NLT).

At Pentecost, the gift of language was the ability to speak in foreign languages (foreign to those in the Upper Room). What was the result? Those with foreign languages said, *"We all hear these people speaking in our own languages..."* (Acts 2:11 NLT). At this time, the gift of languages was for understanding. Later, the gift of tongues seems to be the ability to speak in an unknown language. *"Though I speak with the tongues of men and of angels..."* (1 Cor. 13:1). It seemed to be a supernatural sign.

Today, the problem of language faces each person who seeks to present Jesus Christ cross-culturally. Each culture has its own language, or dialect; each word symbol is filled with meaning and cultural value. Those presenting the Gospel must know the language well enough to make correct language presentations. They need a wide vocabulary and the ability to be fluid in presentation and accurate in pronunciation and articulation.

Jesus has done His part. The Great Commission has been given. Spiritual power is available by the Holy Spirit. The presence of Jesus Christ will go with us. We have a foundational strategy for how to get the job done, and we have the clear objective spelled out. We are to present the Gospel to every person, make disciples, and then baptize them into a church. Finally, we are to teach them to obey all the commands given by Jesus Christ so they will plant another church like the one that reached them with the Gospel.

Our task is to obey the Great Commission by going as He commanded, using every available means at every available time to reach every available person. We must use all our spiritual gifts, having learned them, developed them, and sharpened them. We must implement them in the best way possible to accomplish the most results possible. We must learn the culture we intend to penetrate, knowing the people, their values, and why they live as they do. Then we must baptize new believers into local assemblies that will care for them, teach them, organize them, launch them into service, and resource them so they will complete the Great Commission. Then new believers in new churches must plant another reproducing church like their church. When the last culture is reached and the last man, the Omegan, is brought to salvation, then Jesus Christ will return to wrap up God's eternal plan for the universe and all humanity.

CHAPTER 5

PRINCIPLES FOR CHURCH PLANTING

There seems to be more focus on church planting in the past ten years than at any time in the recent past of church history. Why? Some say it is because American mainline denominations are honestly facing their declining statistics and realizing revitalization is not tied to existing churches but will come by planting new churches.

Other people say that church planting is gaining interest because it grows out of the recent Church Growth Movement of the 1970s and 1980s. That movement emphasizes building a large church (megachurch) to evangelize and/or influence larger areas, usually metropolitan ones. The many reasons for growth and decline in megachurches are discussed at other places. However, individuals are questioning the viability of large churches and suggesting that new church plants are a better solution to reaching a metropolitan area for Christ than bigger and bigger megachurches.

A third reason for new interest in church planting comes from the nature of some large churches. Some are moving into multisite models, that is, one church in multiple locations. This model communicates the central strength of a mother church into satellite churches. All churches in a multisite church have the same DNA and are held together by a single *vision* and a common *value*. These large churches are planting new congregations to ensure continued growth.

Still others see the growth of church planting as a biblical methodology for completing the Great Commission. In the past, some have attempted to carry out the Great Commission by focusing on individuals won to Christ through soul winning, street preaching, mass meetings, and/or media evangelization. But today, many believe the correct biblical methodology is church planting, which may include some of the above methods.

Therefore, many believe the most efficient way to preach the Gospel to every person (Mark 16:15) and to make disciples in every ethnic culture (Matt. 28:18-19) is to plant a reproducing church that will multiply itself into all cultures.

Finally, some believe the key to completing the Great Commission in our generation is when we win the Omegan to Christ. The Omegan will be the last person won to Christ in the last unreached people group or tribe. *"And the Good News about the Kingdom will be preached throughout the whole world, so that all nations will hear it; and then the end will come"* (Matt. 24:14 NLT). They believe when the last tribe is evangelized and the last person is won to Jesus Christ, then the Father will say to the Son, "Go get My people." Then Jesus will come to rapture the church out of the world.

WHY CHURCH PLANTING FAILS

There are many reasons why church planting has failed in the past. One of the main reasons is lack of financing. However, on the flip side, the key to planting a church is never money; it is always purpose and commitment. It's always the power of the Holy Spirit and the sacrificial faith of the people of God. But one of the best reflections of purpose and commitment is money. Because time is money and people show their commitment by sacrificing their money, when there is no money it's an indication people have failed with their commitment to Christ and the project.

Some churches fail because the church planter and/or the team that is going to plant a church has not received the proper biblical training. This usually results in the employment of the wrong authority, the wrong strategy, and/or the wrong methodology. When church planting is based on the biblical principles in the Word of God and the church planter is grounded in the Word of God, church planting can be successful.

The lack of scriptural foundation leads to lack of biblical character. Character in the church planter and planting team can be defined as constantly doing the right (biblical) thing in the right (biblical) manner. When those planting a church lack godly character, that weakness will show up in the new church or will hurt its growth.

Some churches fail due to lack of strategy. People may be praying for a new church and even have a vision of planting a church, but if they do not follow the right strategy the new endeavor will probably fail or proceed slowly.

PASSION → PLANS → STRATEGY → RESULTS →

God anoints and uses leaders according to their commitment to Him as evidenced by their purity of living and their hard work. Any lack of these may erode their effort and destroy it altogether.

This leads to the lack of spiritual maturity. A person can be spiritual immediately by yielding their life to Jesus Christ and walking in total faith. However, spiritual maturity is gained over time; maturity grows when a person constantly seeks the will of God in their life, yields to God's will, and studies the Word of God, and prays. They must learn from their mistakes and successes. That person will grow from their experience and become spiritually mature. It takes mature people to produce a mature church plant.

Finally, church planting will fail from a lack of understanding of the nature of the church. Some new church plants look more like a Christian business than a local church. Some church plants look like an informal Bible study, where people gather around the Word of God. Sometimes a new church looks like a revivalistic prayer meeting and/or any other gathering of Christians for biblical purposes. But a church is the body of Jesus Christ on this earth, and those who plant a church must carry the complete message of Jesus in salvation and sanctification to a needy community. And in doing so, a group of people band together to do corporately what they cannot do individually. They assemble themselves as the local body of Jesus Christ to fulfill all the ministries that Jesus would give to a neighborhood.

WHAT CAN BE LEARNED FROM MISGUIDED EFFORTS?

For ten years, I was executive vice president of Liberty Baptist Fellowship for church planting at Liberty University. Dr. Jerry Falwell was president, and this fellowship was organized to help graduates of Liberty University plant local churches. It followed the example of Dr. Falwell, who had successfully planted Thomas Road Baptist Church in Lynchburg, Virginia. He had saturated the area and built a large church to influence all of Lynchburg, then Central Virginia, next all the Commonwealth of Virginia, then all the United States, and eventually the entire world. The intent of Liberty Baptist Fellowship was to begin local churches all over America like

Thomas Road Baptist Church. Dr. Jerry Falwell Sr. and I had written a book, *Capturing a Town for Christ*, thinking that every church that we planted should capture their town for Christ.[1] During that time, Liberty Baptist Fellowship raised money and planted around 100 local churches.

However, if I were to lead that organization again, I would bring a different emphasis than capturing a town for Christ. If I were to organize a church planting network again, I would make sure that each new church planted by a Liberty graduate would do more than "capture its town for Christ." It should focus on planting multiple churches and/or reproducing churches. The goal would not be to plant just one church but to plant reproducing churches. One church is a limited goal; planting reproducing churches is a limitless goal.

I would do this by motivating church planters to put more emphasis on the Person of Jesus Christ. He attracts non-Christians, transforms their life, and energizes a local assembly to reach lost people. Originally, I put too much emphasis on the doctoral foundation of new churches and not enough emphasis on Jesus.

If I were to run the organization again, I would also put less emphasis on developing organization and programs and would place more emphasis on the local body being an organism of life, vitality, and influence.

Moreover, I would put less emphasis on helping churches find a permanent location, property, and/or buildings. I would emphasize instead making the churches *borderless*. When the Liberty Baptist Fellowship churches focused on land and structures, whether renting or building, too often the size of the new building became a cap on the growth of the new church. Remember, most American churches do not grow beyond the size of their physical facilities.

I would emphasize utilizing rental space and/or donated facilities rather than quickly purchasing facilities. The benefit of renting facilities is that the ministry can eventually move out of small facilities into larger spaces. That would keep the focus on growing the church and reaching more people for Christ.

Also, I would put more emphasis on a vision statement than on a doctoral statement. Vision includes what the church wants to do and its future impact for God. While doctrine is absolutely important and no church can be built without a healthy biblical doctrinal foundation, you must remember that the foundation of any building is usually out of sight. Yes, a church must have a strong foundation, and that is a biblical doctrinal statement. However, what is seen by the world is usually the outward structure, and I would put more emphasis on making the church a reaching, growing community.

Additionally, I would place more emphasis on relationship evangelism rather than door-to-door evangelism or even event evangelism. Too often, churches have prioritized *front-door evangelism*, getting people in the service to present Jesus Christ to them so they will get saved.

New churches should emphasize reaching the lost through relationship evangelism—evangelism carried out through family, friends, and business acquaintances. A new church should have an aggressive witness and testimony to unsaved neighbors.

I would focus new church plants on their ministry of evangelism, discipleship, service, and fellowship. Each church attracts people primarily by who they are and what they do, not by their organization and programs. The more a church ministers to its neighborhood, the more it carries out the Great Commission of Jesus Christ.

ADVANTAGES IN CHURCH PLANTING

Because Jesus Christ is the church that assembles on this earth as His body, then we must see the sovereign grace and mercy of

God in every church plant. It is not about doing something for God; it is God partnering with people as they attempt to carry out His will. Church planting is never just human will; it is the will of God through humans.

Realize that the ultimate vision of evangelism is carried out by church planting. Everything a main church must do it does when planting a new assembly.

The job of evangelizing a community is far beyond the investment of time and resources. All of that is necessary, but church planting involves prayer and fasting, where God's presence and power are called upon. When God becomes evident in the process, His power flows through all the people of the church to touch the lives of unsaved people in the community.

There must be a comprehensive and biblical strategy to partner with God in influencing a community. Because the church is Jesus Christ, the best way to influence a community is to plant Jesus in their midst.

Sometimes evangelism by media, that is, either radio or television, is randomly sowing seeds, hoping that some seeds will be planted in the hearts of the unsaved and they will get saved. The same with Christian literature distribution and/or door-to-door evangelism. All these forms of evangelism are necessary and good; however, planting a church requires precision planting and focused growth, which lead to a biblical harvest.

Compare sowing seeds at random on a plot of ground to target planting an area with a specific seed at a specific time. The latter begins with selecting a plot of ground, preparing the soil, removing weeds and rocks, planting seed at the right time in the year and at the right distance from one another in the earth, then watering it by prayer and Bible study, and seeing God bring forth a harvest.

There is a logical progress in church planting. First, you plant the seeds in the hearts of unsaved people, then win them to Jesus Christ, and next disciple them for Christian maturity. New believers must become part of the assembly, that is, congregationalized. Then the new believers must be trained and recruited for service. Finally, when individuals are serving the Lord, that produces more seed that leads to another church plant.

The best place to train people for church planting is by planting a church. While some training can be done by learning the theory and principles of church planting, those who actually begin a church learn how to do it, and they can be used to begin another church the same way. This means that the practical experience they gained in serving the Lord can translate into ongoing discipleship as they help plant another church.

TYPES OF CHURCH PLANTING

The following is a list of various types of church planting. Please note that it is not a comprehensive list. I don't recommend each of the following strategies but have included them for comparative value.

1. *Parenting a new church.* The church in Jerusalem planted another church in Samaria. When believers left Jerusalem to go to Samaria, they technically planted another church. *"But the believers who were scattered preached the Good News about Jesus wherever they went. Philip, for example, went to the city of Samaria and told the people there about the Messiah"* (Acts 8:4-5 NLT).

2. *Planting a new reproducing church.* When each new church plants another church, this is church multiplication. This has primarily been the plan for churches throughout Western Christianity. They follow the pattern found in Scripture. *"The church at Antioch of*

Syria...after more fasting and prayer, the men laid their hands on them [Paul and Barnabas] *and sent them on their way"* (Acts 13:1,3 NLT).

3. *Planting multisite churches.* This is one church starting many local churches and extending its governance and its DNA to each newly planted church by *vision* and *value*. The church at Jerusalem apparently was a multisite church. The Jerusalem church was described as multitudes, plural (see Acts 4:32), but at the same time it was described as a multitude, singular (see Acts 6:5). This suggests that the church at Jerusalem had two centers or foci. The first was the temple, where they met together for worship and celebration. The second was all the individual homes, where they met together for Bible study, prayer, and the celebration of the Lord's Table. *"And every day, in the Temple and from house to house, they continued to teach and preach this message: 'Jesus is the Messiah'"* (Acts 5:42 NLT). Jerusalem had one main congregation that met in the temple, but it also had many (multisite) meetings in the homes of believers.

Also, the use of the word *house* or *home* in Romans 16 suggests there was a church in Rome, that is, one large church (see Rom. 16:10-23). However, it was located in many homes. There was a church in the home of Aquila and Priscilla, plus three or four other names were mentioned. Finally, the reference to *"the churches of Christ"* suggests that this was a predominately Jewish home church because emphasis was put on Jesus, the predicted Messiah who would come (Rom. 16:16). Then Paul concludes the chapter by greeting *"the whole church"* (Rom. 16:23). This suggests that the church in Rome could have been a multisite church.

4. *Church planting by fusion.* This is when several small churches become one church. There comes a time when difficulties result from population shifts, the closing of industries, aging clientele, causing

churches to struggle. Fusion occurs when several struggling churches join together to become a new church that is larger and stronger.

5. *District team church planting.* This is when several churches in an area join together to plant one local church. Usually this one church is not part of any of the existing churches but is a separate, independent, indigenous church (self-supporting, self-governing, and self-producing).

6. *Becoming a satellite church.* This is when a smaller church associates with a larger church or group of other churches but retains its independent governance. This could represent an embryonic denomination or fellowship or network of churches. The Baptist Bible Fellowship of Springfield, Missouri, includes a number of like-faith and like-practice churches that join together in fellowship for strength and outreach in planting new churches.

7. *Task force church planting.* This is when a denomination and/ or mission agency plants one church, usually one at a time. Today in Manila, the capital of the Philippines, Global Surge, under the direction of Greg Lyons, has planted around 30 churches in the past 15 years. Lyons is a missionary from the Baptist Bible Fellowship who planted Asia Baptist Bible College (about 1,500 students) to train young people in church ministry. This ministry is connected to Camp Highlands, an evangelistic camp where young people from the streets are given a camping experience with the purpose of meeting Jesus Christ as Savior. They return to Manila to be trained in a Bible college and become part of planting a new local church. Global Surge purposes not to own church facilities and/or develop church programs, but rather to build and plant indigenous churches that function with the ministries of Bible study, evangelism, prayer, and fellowship.

PLANTING A CHURCH LIKE YOUR CHURCH

When church planting takes place, the seed that forms the new church is taken from an existing church. Usually the DNA of an existing church becomes the life thread that develops a new satellite church. The two churches become similar in doctrine, purpose, belief, but most of all in practice.

Therefore, to understand church planting, look at the six dominant types of local churches found in Western Christianity. This list reflects six ways churches worship or produce Christianity. Their practice becomes a most important influence in a new church. When new churches are planted, these six church types are usually reflected in their new plants.

1. *The evangelistic church.* Some local churches have a dominant evangelistic lifestyle that gives focus and meaning to the life of the church. When they meet for prayer, they are usually praying for evangelistic outreach. The same thing happens in worship services and in ministry projects—evangelism is typically their focus. Many churches give an invitation for salvation at the end of a Gospel service; others have outreach programs where people go door-to-door or have planned visitation soul winning. These churches may teach soul winning programs such as Evangelism Explosion, the Four Spiritual Laws, or the Roman Road to Salvation.

One such church that is known to be seeker driven is Willow Creek Church in Chicago, Illinois, led by Pastor Bill Hybels. This church seeks to present Jesus Christ to lost people. Saddleback Church in Orange County, California, led by Pastor Rick Warren, calls itself seeker sensitive. It does not present the Gospel in all of its services but rather is always very sensitive to attempt to win lost people to Christ.

In the past 100 years, Southern Baptist churches in the United States have primarily been evangelistic churches, focusing on soul winning visitation, Gospel altar calls during Sunday services, and showing a passion for reaching lost people.

The spiritual gift represented in these churches is evangelism, as seen in Paul's statement, *"And He Himself gave some to be apostles, some prophets, some evangelists, and some pastors and teachers"* (Eph. 4:11). The dominant gift of the pastors of these churches is evangelism.

2. *The Bible-teaching church.* The dominant characteristic of these churches is expositional teaching from the pulpit. People may carry study Bibles, and many bring notebooks to church to take notes on the sermon. The pastor may distribute a printed outline and/or use PowerPoints for instruction and notetaking by the congregation. There are many churches illustrating this method, for example, the First Baptist Church of Atlanta, Georgia, pastored by Charles Stanley, an expositional teacher. Chuck Smith, who began Calvary Chapel, was noted for teaching through the Bible from Genesis to Revelation in a verse-by-verse manner. Also, John MacArthur of Grace Community Church in Sun Valley, California, is noted for his expositional teaching. The MacArthur Study Bible is perhaps one of the best study Bibles available.

The dominant spiritual gift in this type of church is teaching (see Eph. 4:11). When Paul designates spiritual gifts in Romans 12, he says, *"...If you are a teacher, teach well"* (Rom. 12:7 NLT). Again, when Paul begins to list the spiritual gifts, he states, *"Here are some of the parts God has appointed for the church...third are teachers..."* (1 Cor. 12:28 NLT).

3. *The exhortation church.* The dominant characteristic of this church type is positive motivational preaching (as opposed to negative). People are challenged to godly living and godly service.

The exhortation church is modeled by the Christ Fellowship Church in Palm Beach Gardens, Florida, first by the founding pastor, Tom Mullins, and now his son, Todd Mullins, who presently leads the church. The dominant gift of the pastor is exhorting individuals to godly living and Christian service.

The spiritual gift for this church is the gift of encouragement and/or exhortation. *"If your gift is to encourage others, be encouraging..."* (Rom. 12:8 NLT).

4. *The body-life church.* This is the church of small groups and/ or relationships. A pastor who began a cell in the greater Seattle, Washington, area said, "Our church does not have small groups; our church is small groups." Pastor Yonggi Cho of the Full Gospel Church in Seoul, Korea, said, "Everything the church is supposed to do we do in small groups...we study the Bible, worship, sing, fellowship, collect an offering, and pray for one another and encourage one another."

In the 1950s, the largest church in the world was the First Baptist Church of Dallas, Texas, with Dr. W.A. Criswell as its pastor. He built the church on small Sunday school classes with about ten students each. These small classes did not represent the total church ministry, as Cho explained above, but they were focused on teaching the Word of God at each appropriate grade level. However, the lay Sunday school teacher was seen as a substitute pastor. As Cho stated, "Everything the pastor is to the larger flock the Sunday school teacher is to their Sunday school flock."

The dominant characteristics of body-life churches are relationships and service. These churches may use the symbol of the basin and towel to characterize their ministry, following the example of Jesus: *"And since I, your Lord and Teacher, have washed your feet, you ought to wash each other's feet"* (John 13:14 NLT).

Their spiritual gift is ministering or serving one another. Paul notes, *"If your gift is serving others, serve them well..."* (Rom. 12:7 NLT). This gift is characterized by sympathy (feeling for people) and empathy (feeling with people).

5. *The liturgical or worshiping church.* The dominant characteristic of the liturgical church is planned, focused worship. This church historically would use devotional sermons, responsive readings, doxologies, organ and/or piano music, and hymns ending with "Amen."

The characteristic of the contemporary liturgical church is praise worship, lifted hands, a praise band with electric support, spontaneous shouts of "amen" and "hallelujah," and in some churches, speaking in tongues.

An illustration of the contemporary liturgical church is Hillsong Church in Sydney, Australia. The typical Lutheran, Presbyterian, or Episcopal worship services would illustrate traditional liturgical worship.

Howard Hendricks at Dallas Theological Seminary often said, "Worship is the lost cord of Christianity." And what is worship? It comes from the old Scottish term *worthship*, which means "giving the worth to God that is due to Him." Perhaps the best verse to illustrate worship is Psalms 22:3: *"Yet you are holy, enthroned on the praises of Israel"* (NLT).

Some have seen the restoration of contemporary worship and the revitalization of historic worship as indicators that we are in the last days of Christianity. They justify their view from the Scriptures, which state: *"I will restore the fallen tabernacle of David...so that the rest of humanity might seek the Lord"* (see Acts 15:16-17). The word *tabernacle* has always been associated with Moses; it was Moses's tabernacle. There was never a tabernacle of David. Yet during David's lifetime, the tabernacle for sacrifice and offerings was located down near the

Pool of Siloam outside of Jerusalem's walls. At the same time, part of the tabernacle was located on Mount Zion, where the presence of God was. Worshipers would gather to praise the Lord with lifted hands: *"...all you servants of the Lord, you who serve at night in the house of the Lord. Lift your hands toward the sanctuary, and praise the Lord"* (Ps. 134:1-2 NLT). Many see the contemporary outpouring of worship as the fulfillment of Scripture, which says that in the last days, the tabernacle of David will be raised up.

6. *The congregational church.* This is the church of the people, by the people, and for the people. The dominant characteristics are lay preaching, lay leadership, and lay ministry. Many times, when pastors are not available, laymen take the lead. Also, many churches choose not to call full-time pastors but use lay people in their leadership ministry. The Jotabeche Church in Santiago, Chile, is one large mother church that has multiple satellite churches—one cathedral downtown and approximately 20 churches called temples in surrounding areas, each led by a layman. Beyond that, they have another 80 groups that are called churches; they too are led by lay people.

There are many illustrations of the congregational church throughout history: Brethren, Puritans, Pilgrims. Today, the dominant illustration is the house church of China.

What is the spiritual gift of the congregational church? Leadership. *"...If God has given you leadership ability, take the responsibility seriously..."* (Rom. 12:8 NLT).

The point of this section is that evangelistic churches plant churches that minister like them, that is, evangelistically. The same goes for the other types of churches. Exhorting churches plant churches that exhort. Body-life churches plant churches that have cells. Liturgical churches plant churches that are focused on worship. To determine how a new church will minister, look at the mother church.

TEN ELEMENTS OF CHURCH PLANTING

1. *Prayer.* At no time or place can we separate prayer from any ministry on this earth. Prayer is the strategical master plan for reaching any new people group. Before planting a church, people must be given to prayer, and the neighborhood must be saturated in prayer. Beyond that, all plans must be covered by prayer.

Early in the transfer of vision and values to the new church, prayer becomes the road by which the transfer is made. All momentum for any new church plant will come from prayer.

2. *Abundant Gospel sowing.* There can be no church planting without evangelism. Without it, all new works will struggle. Mission churches and Sunday school missions have been planted, and God has blessed the teaching of the Word of God, but without evangelism outreach to lost people, there is no new life and enduring ministry. Only as a church sows the Gospel with abundant faith will it reap abundant harvest. God has said, *"...You will always harvest what you plant"* (Gal. 6:7 NLT).

3. *Intentional church planting.* The key to successful church planting is based on a deliberate effort to begin a new church with all its ministries. Churches don't simply happen, just as farm land doesn't automatically produce a great harvest. There must be an intention to plant a church with the purpose of evangelizing an area and fulfilling the command of Jesus Christ. Intentionality leads to strategy, and strategy leads to plans, dates, locations, and activities.

4. *Spiritual authority.* The Bible must be the guiding source for doctrine, strategy, polity, and even church life itself. Because the Bible has life and gives life, any church endeavor that is not based on the Word of God will not have life, nor will it have any long-term results. The Bible gives purpose and direction for the new church.

5. *Leadership.* John Maxwell has often said, "Everything rises and falls on leadership." Therefore, there must be a leader and/or leadership team in every new church plant.

In the 1950s, one of the greatest church planting sources was Baptist Bible College in Springfield, Missouri. The president of the college, Dr. G.B. Vick, often said, "Great men plant great churches, average men grow average churches, and weak men cannot plant churches, but in the end those churches plateau or decline."

The strength of the new church plants depends on the total life and ministry of its leader. If the leader is committed to evangelism, the church will probably be evangelistic. If the leader is committed to Bible knowledge and teaching, the church will be a strong great Bible center. If the leader is great in exhortation and motivation, the church will be motivated to serve God. If the leader has the heart of worship, the new church will be a worshiping church. The new church will grow according to the leadership seed that is planted.

6. *Lay leadership.* The growing edge of any new church is first the leader or leadership team, and then lay people will carry out the ministry. Obviously, there must be a great leader to lead great churches. But great leaders can never do it alone; they must delegate and recruit other leaders to serve with them. The reliance upon lay leadership will ensure that the new church will succeed because out of it will come the growth and multiplication of ministry, evangelism, abundant life, and maturity.

7. *New church outreach by planting a new church.* The secret of a great future for any church is when it plans to start another church like itself. When God created life, He put its "seed within" so that plant life would reproduce itself. He did the same for animal life and human beings. The "seed within" was God's strategy for the reproduction and multiplication of life.

The first church planters were laymen. *"But the believers who were scattered preached the Good News about Jesus wherever they went"* (Acts 8:4 NLT). The next wave of church planters were Barnabas and Saul, who were sent out from the Antioch church (see Acts 13:1-3). Today, foreign missionaries and/or church planting pastors are sent out to begin new churches.

The exponential phase of reproduction began when new churches began themselves to plant other new churches. *"This went on for the next two years, so that people throughout the province of Asia—both Jews and Greeks—heard the Word of the Lord"* (Acts 19:10 NLT).

8. *Rapid growth.* The wonderful thing about new churches is that they are unencumbered with nonessential elements. It seems that the longer a church exists, the more programs, organizations, and committees it finds and uses. Many of these new "things" are not primarily life-sustaining and reproducing. We must evaluate things that are added to the church that are not vital yet contribute to its ministry. Space is necessary in new facilities, new programs give new life, and new officers and workers add abundance to the ministry. The fact that something could be dropped without endangering the mission of the church indicates that it was never essential to the church's life in the first place.

9. *Healthy churches.* Every seed that is planted must grow into a healthy plant before it can produce a harvest. Although leaves, stalks, and branches do not necessarily bear fruit, there would be no harvest without them. While not seed-bearing, all of them—leaves, stalks, and branches—make for a healthy plant. And healthy plants bring forth a great harvest. Therefore, in a local church, make sure you always give priority to the essential aspects, but never ignore the nonessential ones.

THE ABSOLUTE ESSENTIALS

When the early human race was threatened by sexual sins, God found a servant—Noah—to save the world.

When the nations were given over to idolatry, God found a servant—Abraham—to worship the one true God.

When the world faced seven years of severe famine, God found a servant—Joseph—to save Egypt and the world.

God has always had His servants to attain the unattainable, remove barriers, and do the supernatural. Whether the servant was named Samuel, or Deborah, or David, or Nehemiah, or Paul, God has always used a person.

Remember, a new church is always planted by a person, but it is never built on a person.

A new church is always caused, but it is never caused by a person; it is caused by God.

Although God does not use a modern Gideon to slay an army of Midianites, God still uses the same principles of faith and obedience, along with His power, to bring about a victory.

Dr. Vick once told me, "If a young man wants to plant a church that will be influential, he must study great men." Learning from those who have planted successful churches will give many insights to the church planter who wants to build a powerful new church for the glory of God.

Remember Philippians 4:13: *"I can do all things [which He has called me to do] through Him who strengthens and empowers me"* (AMP).

CHAPTER 6

PRINCIPLES FOR THE CHURCH PLANTER

The one who decides to plant a church is usually motivated by the "impossible dream." Because the church is the Body of Christ, it is God's supernatural tool to stop evil and invade satan's dominion to capture souls for Jesus Christ. Because the church is Jesus, it is never a human invention, nor is it a human accomplishment; it is God at work in the world. The correctly planted church is the presence of Jesus in the world, capturing lost souls in the grips of hell, releasing them by the power of Jesus, and then empowering them to do that same work in other lost people. Therefore, planting a force this powerful is something humans can't do by themselves—it's an impossible dream.

A church is a "called-out group" made up of those who leave the world and commit themselves to follow Jesus Christ. Because Christ indwells each believer, they come together to form His body on earth so that the presence of Jesus Christ fills the church. They are "called out" from the normal pursuits of life to carry out the Great Commission. The church is established by God, empowered by God, and ultimately God is its objective. Therefore, those who would plant a church must be empowered by Christ, who is its founder.

The world does not love the church. As a matter of fact, those who reject God will reject the church planter and fight against the church He plans to build. Think about it: the normal human is motivated by the desire to protect himself, to gain riches for himself, and to find pleasure for himself. But when a person plants a church, he is going against the tide of self-interest. He is saying, *"...not I, but Christ..."* (Gal. 2:20 KJV).

A church is not a business; the American business scene is dominated by both moral and immoral people. The success of business is measured by the bottom line, showing a profit, or making money. But the bottom line of churches is not showing a financial profit. It's about carrying out the commands of Jesus to go into all the world, win lost people to salvation, and then teach them to go out and repeat the process, that is, win more lost people to Jesus.

The world hates Christian influence and will not naturally embrace a new church. Why? Because the church stands against everything the world stands for. Therefore, God must perform a miracle each time a new church is planted. That miracle will give life to individuals and influence a neighborhood and/or its culture.

Into this improbable situation steps a church planter. The Scriptures teach, *"There was a man sent from God, whose name was John"* (John 1:6). God has always sought for a person who will stand in the gap (see Ezek. 22:30). God is always looking for an Isaiah who will say, *"Here am I! Send me"* (Isa. 6:8). Therefore, God is looking for a church planter to make a difference in the neighborhood where the church is planted.

One of the greatest accomplishments in life is when a person or group of people start a New Testament church that influences people and neighborhoods for Christ. It begins with obedience to God's call to present the Gospel to lost people, and it continues as the church is planted and grows and as new believers are baptized and taught to obey all things that Jesus has taught us.

Because planting the church is an "unattainable task," the church planter needs the power of Christ to accomplish it. The new church is never planted by a man, nor is it built on a man, but it is built on Jesus Christ. Committees do not build churches; neither are churches started by a written declaration or even a public announcement. The church is begun in the heart of a church planter or team of church planters, and it grows through fasting and sacrificial labor. Churches begin to appear when the power of Jesus Christ fills servants and flows through them to touch unsaved people.

Remember, a great church is always caused; it never just happens. God always has His servant who will sacrifice, pray, and work to build the church of Jesus Christ.

The church planter driving his U-Haul truck into a new neighborhood is about as formidable as David standing before Goliath with five smooth stones. This is the thesis of this book—that God still uses the average man, with limited resources, against insurmountable obstacles, in unlikely circumstances, to build a church for the glory of God.

Although God does not use a modern Joshua to conquer the physical land of promise, He still uses the same principles. When a church is planted, God indwells the man/woman who stands with the Word of God against a daunting foe so that he/she is filled with the Holy Spirit, empowered by the Word of God, strengthened by prayer, and empowered to do the will of God.

Some church plants fail simply because the leaders were not spirit filled, nor did they have well-balanced principles. They did not have faith, nor did they apply the principles of the Word of God. Simply, the new church failed because the leadership did not follow the basic ingredients of Christianity to build a new church.

To plant an influential church, leaders must have a hard-headed tenacity, declaring, "I will never give up." They believe with Paul, *"I can do all things through Christ that strengthens me"* (Phil. 4:13). And they breathed the prayer, *"For to me, to live is Christ, and to die is gain"* (Phil. 1:21).

Yes, the church planter must be determined, but he must also develop the meekness of the Puritans, who planted a new colony when they set foot in Massachusetts. They realized their strength was in God, not in themselves.

The church planter must have a reverence for things spiritual yet possess the calculating eye of a businessman who can read a financial statement and balance a church budget.

Church planters must be quick to learn, quick to adapt, and quick to acquire knowledge in a thousand areas where they are ignorant. Yet at the same time, they must lead authoritatively, for no one else can or will lead the church.

The church planter must speak persuasively in public yet listen sympathetically in private counsel.

The church planter must have an iron will, wide scholarship, unblemished experience, and a willingness to experiment, yet be committed to tried and workable principles and never give up. If he does not have it all when he begins, he must gain it quickly, and in the process of acquiring these skills, he will plant a church that will influence a community for the glory of God. He must grow spiritually in relationship to the requirements of his vision. In one sense, he will never plant or establish a church as influential as he seeks, but he will always strive to obtain the unattainable so that he might build to the glory of God.

As Daniel stood before the lions…

As David slew his 10,000…

As Elijah stood alone on Mount Carmel…

Today, the church planter must go forth to establish a church.

IS THERE A GIFT OF CHURCH PLANTING?

What do we know about spiritual gifts? First of all, we receive our spiritual gifts embryonically at the time of salvation. Then after we are saved and are following Christ, our gifts begin to appear and grow in effectiveness and strengthen themselves. Finally, when a God-called person assumes a church leadership position, his gifts are recognized and validated.

The spiritual gift of evangelism must be included in church planting. *"Now these are the gifts Christ gave to the church: the apostles, the prophets, the evangelists, and the pastors and teachers. Their responsibility is to equip God's people to do his work and build up the church, the body of Christ"* (Eph. 4:11-12 NLT).

The spiritual gift that will be used most in planting a church is evangelism. This gift is evidenced in a burden to win souls and a manifest ability to relate to lost people and point them to Christ. The fruit of evangelism is when souls are won to Jesus Christ (see John 15:16). We have seen the gift of evangelism manifested in those who held citywide or local church evangelistic crusades. But it is also evident in foreign and home missionaries who preach the Gospel in unevangelized areas with the view of establishing churches to fulfill the Great Commission.

If church planting is not a spiritual gift, then the church planter or group planting a new church must use all the spiritual resources available to them, meaning applying every spiritual gift in their endeavor to plant a new church.

The term *evangelist* is only mentioned three times in the New Testament. In Acts 21:8, Phillip was called "an evangelist" because he carried out the Great Commission to places where there was no Gospel. Second, Timothy was told to do the work of an evangelist (see 2 Tim. 4:5). Third, evangelism appears in a list of spiritual gifts after being an apostle (to establish the Gospel) and being a prophet (to speak the Word of God). That means the evangelist receives his message from the apostles and prophets who wrote Scripture, then passes the message onto others.

The root meaning of the word *evangelist* is "to bring good tidings" or "to gospelize." Therefore, an evangelist goes to an area or to a people who have never been evangelized. He preaches or gives the Gospel to them. Then, after some get saved, he assembles new believers together and disciples them in their new Christian faith.

In one sense, those with the gift of evangelism will have a special ability to win people to Christ, more so than the average Christian. Because spiritual gifts are both qualitative and quantitative, the gift of evangelism will have a deeper grip on those with the gift than on the average Christian who is not dominated with this gift. Then, in a quantitative way, they will probably lead more to Jesus Christ than other believers.

To illustrate this point, I believe I have the gift of teaching, and Jerry Falwell Sr., who planted Thomas Road Baptist Church, had the gift of evangelism. If both of us were exposed to or preached to the same audience in a church, and we both preached and gave an invitation for people to receive Jesus Christ as Savior, I believe Jerry would win more people to Christ out of that audience that I could.

Therefore, let's describe the gift of evangelism. It begins with a spiritual burden for lost people. The one with this gift will pray and seek God's power to present salvation and communicate the Gospel to the unsaved. This gift comes from a vision he/she has for people and for what God can do in an area. Therefore, more than anyone else, the church planter with the gift of evangelism will have a vision for planting a church in an area. He/she will have a deeper desire to evangelize than other Christians.

THE CALL TO CHURCH PLANTING

If any person is called to ministry, it involves a threefold aspect. First of all, the call of God involves a burden. The church planter feels, "I *must* go and plant a church." Second, the call of God is manifested in a desire: "I *want* to plant a church more than anything else." The third reflection of the call of God is fruit. God uses those He calls in an unusual way to bring forth fruit. *"You didn't choose Me. I chose you. I appointed you to go and produce lasting fruit, so that the Father will give you whatever you ask for, using My name"* (John 15:16 NLT).

Look at Paul, who was called of God into full-time Christian service. At his conversion, he was set aside for ministry. God told Ananias, *"Go, for Saul is My chosen instrument to take My message to the Gentiles and to kings, as well as to the people of Israel. And I will show him how much he must suffer for My name's sake"* (Acts 9:15-16 NLT).

The second step in Paul's call was seen when he was fasting and praying with the leadership at the church in Antioch. The Holy Spirit said, *"Appoint Barnabas and Saul for the special work to which I have called them"* (Acts 13:2 NLT). Then Paul and Barnabas actively responded and went to Cyrus to begin preaching the Gospel. People were saved, and a church was established. This is the fruit of God's call on their life.

Remember, no person can aspire to be called of God, and no one decides to become a servant of Jesus Christ. *"...Paul, a slave of Christ Jesus,* [was] *chosen by God to be an apostle..."* (Rom. 1:1 NLT).

When a person is called of God, there must be soul searching so that the recipient finds the mind of the Lord and has an assurance in his heart that God has called him to be a minister.

When I am ordaining a young person for ministry, I always ask two questions. "First, tell me how you know that you are called of God. If you don't have that absolute assurance, I will vote against you today." The candidate will usually describe the nature of the call, for example, first, a burden that he must preach; and second, a desire to preach; and third, evidence of how God has used him to bring fruit in his life.

A second question: "If this council does not vote to ordain you, what will you do?" If a candidate is really called of God, he will determine to go preach and serve the Lord out of obedience to God, rather than give up because a council didn't ordain him.

There are two or three things about a call that you must know. Some people are called immediately when they are converted, but others are not called until they have grown in their walk with Jesus Christ. Over the years, I have asked this question in classes at Liberty University, and I have found that about 10 percent of the students were called when they were converted. About 90 percent were called later in their Christian journey.

Another question I have asked is how the call came to them. Again, about 10 percent received a call from God suddenly in one great experience in which they see God's intent for their life. This is illustrated by turning on a light in a dark room so a person will suddenly see everything. At the same time, about 90 percent feel the call came gradually. Just as there is a little light that precedes the sun's emergence over the horizon, so gradually some people begin to see the plan of God for their life. Slowly they feel God leading them into full-time Christian service.

The issue is not whether you were called by God gradually or suddenly in one life-changing experience. Also, it's not about where you were called, when you were converted to Christ, etc. The issue is the call of God.

THE MANAGEMENT STYLE OF THE CHURCH PLANTER

The church planter will be like the self-made business person. He must be a growing individual, knowing that over a period of time his role will change. He will plant a church and organize it, slowly developing it to maturity. With time he will submit himself to the organization he began and work for that organization he grew, realizing that the new church organization is greater than him, for it is the work of Jesus Christ in the world.

That means that the church planter begins by taking responsibility for every aspect of the church. He is accountable to the church, doing everything and anything necessary to build the new church. However, over a period of time he gives away his authority; deacons are appointed and other committees are formed. The church planter now shares his authority with other groups in the church and eventually submits himself to their authority.

Another way of looking at pastoral leadership is that the church planter begins with a structured downward cycle of management. The business leader is a pioneer, personal manager, worker, motivator, and visiting fireman to solve problems, all wrapped up in one personality. Therefore, the pastor is like a business owner; in reality, he is the life of the business. In that sense, the business and the businessman are inseparable, and so the pastor and the church are inseparable. The church planter becomes the church, and all the while he realizes that Jesus is the church and it is Jesus who indwells him, working through him to build the church.

After a church/company has existed for a length of time, new needs arise. A different type of management is needed. The pastor/

business leader who started it and manages its growth now must move toward a bottom-up management strategy. What does this mean? A top-down structure of governance must change as the organization grows. In the early days of a local church, the pastor conceived ideas relating to the church and introduced them to the people and then oversaw their implementation. However, after a period of time, that cycle is reversed to an upward cycle of leadership. That means the pastor shares his ideas with committees or groups of people. He plants innovative ideas in the minds of the people so that the committees understand what is necessary to make changes, or the people in the church themselves want to see innovation and propose ideas. Within that period of time, the upward cycle of authority develops. This builds loyalty on the part of the people to the church. In the early days, much of the church's loyalty is evidenced as the people followed the pastor. But in later days, loyalties are transferred to the church.

This is not only natural; it is therapeutic as well. An upward cycle of management will curb any rebellious attitudes of people to authority within the church. The people must constantly feel that this is "my church," not "the pastor's church."

The highly structured downward cycle forces change throughout the system. However, the upward cycle of management builds team loyalty, team ownership, and team motivation. This means the people stop doing things for the pastor, and they begin doing things with the pastor. Then eventually they appreciate the pastor doing things for them. Finally, they do things instead of the pastor.

So, what happens when we have an upward cycle of leadership? The group/church becomes the standard for individual conformity. The church planter is no longer the standard. Therefore, people begin to live as others in the Body of Christ; therefore, the Body of Christ becomes the standard.

Proper individual behavior will slowly become internalized with the upward cycle of leadership. People began to feel, "This is the way Christians act. This is the way I act."

The final benefit of the upward cycle is that it motivates individuals to improve themselves and ultimately to improve the local church.

Note the difference. When a pastor plants a church, he begins with the downward cycle of leadership. However, if that same pastor goes to a church in existence, he must assume an upward cycle of leadership. That pastor, when he moves from a church plant to an existing church, must assume a different strategy in leading the next church.

But sometimes pastors leave a church plant and assume the downward cycle when they go to an existing church. What happens? He may split the congregation because some are used to an upward cycle of leadership and rebel against his downward cycle. Second, he could lose certain members who will leave the church individually or as a group. Third, the church could vote the pastor out because of his domineering downward cycle of leadership.

STRENGTH OF THE PIONEERING METHOD OF CHURCH PLANTING

The first great strength is the fact that the churches get started because pioneers paid the price to get them started. A second strength is that the pastor has great liberty in the upward cycle of church growth. But note the opposite can also be true: a pastor might attempt an "upward cycle" of leadership with a church plant, but it may falter and fail due to his lack of leadership.

Usually, a new church will be as strong as the ability of the pastor who is planting the church. As Hosea said, *"Like priest, like church"* (see Hosea 4:9). Churches will take on both the strengths and the weaknesses of the church planter. Therefore, as quickly as possible, the church planter must change his strategy from the downward cycle of leadership to the upward cycle of leadership.

CONCLUSION

Some have asked, "Is there an ideal personality type for a church planter?" Some think the church planter must be a rough individualist who can persevere in spite of the odds. Others think he must be a charismatic personality who attracts people to himself; hence, he builds churches on his personality. Still others think the church planter must understand delegation, knowing how to motivate other people to work.

However, God has used all types of leaders to plant New Testament churches. There have been aggressive leaders who have gone out and planted the church on their hard work and determination. Jerry Falwell Sr. made 100 house calls a day, 5 days a week. He followed that practice daily until he had personally gone to every house in a 10-mile radius of his local church.

On the other hand, there are missionaries who work through local leaders and don't plant one church, but many. Missionary Lonnie Smith in Monterrey, Mexico, planted over 30 churches by working through individuals to plant each one.

Whether the church planter will plant one church by his persistence or hundreds of churches, God uses leaders according to their ability.

Since Jesus is the founder of the church, He uses humans who are dedicated to Him to plant His church. Only Jesus Christ can accentuate a person's talents to plant a church. At the same time, God compensates for weaknesses so that inadequate individuals with meager abilities and marginal talents can build a church to the glory of

God. When the church planter is God's servant, he has the ability to overcome insurmountable odds, solve problems, and accomplish the supernatural work of God.

Church planters must be pioneers; however, only certain people have that trait. They must be willing to swing the hammer while also negotiating financing for long-term resources. They must be able to motivate from the pulpit while at the same time persuading people on an individual basis. Church planters must be able to preach, counsel, rebuke, and teach the Word of God. They must be able to do it all, for they usually begin with little or no help. They must be able to recruit, share a vision, and motivate people to help them complete the project of building the church. They must nurture followers, train them in service, and inspire them to spiritual greatness.

Remember, in Scripture some planted, some nurtured, and some watered, but always God gave the fruit (see 1 Cor. 3:1-7). The church planter must be humble, realizing that it is God who works through his abilities, no matter how strong or weak.

A church planter must have vision, as did the prophets of the Old Testament called "seers" (see 1 Sam. 9:9). That means he must have the eyes of God, seeing things first, seeing furthest into the future, and seeing the most that God can do.

The church planter must have faith to believe that God can complete the project that is in his heart. He sees the church on the street corner before he begins to draw plans on paper. He must have faith to win souls to Christ, raise money, arrange for a location, and do a thousand other details to make a local church happen.

The church planter must have courage to face discouragement, disappointment, and people who turn their backs on him and the church. Even when the church does not grow as rapidly as he expected or the facilities are not as elaborate as he desired, he needs courage to accept the present limitations without losing faith, never letting the present rob the future.

The church planter must have passion, building the church on the love of God flowing through him. He must love people, including those who criticize him. He must pray for all people that they will become saved and bring glory to God. He must never allow bitterness to sour his attitude, but in all things, he must be known as a person of love.

The church planter needs tenacity to build a successful church. He cannot build a church without presiding over hardships, disappointments, and failures. He must never give up. Planting a church is an endless struggle, and because he senses God's call to community, he does not turn back because of opposition. He does not get discouraged because of trials. Because he has a burden from God for the area in which he is planting a church, he rejects any temptation to go to a settled pastorate elsewhere and look for a bigger salary. He must be like Jesus, who *"steadfastly set His face to go to Jerusalem"* (Luke 9:51). He must commit himself to building the church because he made a promise to God and himself that he would do it.

The church planter must embody all of the qualities of the Christian life because he is the shepherd of the flock and is an example to all.

The church planter must be filled with the Spirit, empowered by the Spirit, and controlled by the Spirit in his preaching, teaching, soul winning, and management of all the details of the church.

This leads to the fruit of the Spirit in his personal life (see Gal. 5:22-23). In short, he must simply be "God's person," called to that area to plant a church for the glory of God.

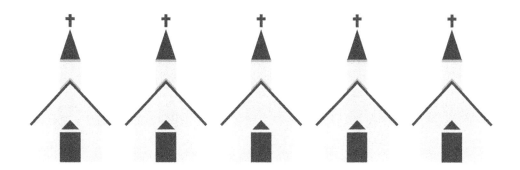

Part Two

TYPES OF CHURCH PLANTING: A LOOK AT VARIOUS TYPES OF CHURCH PLANTING

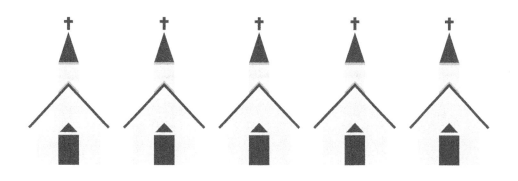

CHAPTER 7

PLANTING Multisite CHURCHES

Many claim that the Seacoast Church in the greater Charleston, South Carolina, area was the first example of a multisite church in the United States (at least the first publicly recognized one in recent history).

Seacoast Church did not immediately intend to begin a satellite ministry, but rather circumstances backed it into satellite services. The church met in the Mount Pleasant community, which is located on a series of coastal islands surrounded by creeks and marshes. There was only one road and one two-lane bridge into the community. Seacoast had purchased and operated on 14 acres of ground. God was blessing the outreach, and a number of people were coming from outside of the island community to attend the church. The one road and bridge were saturated on Sundays. The church grew to two morning services, then launched a Saturday night worship service.

When the church planned to build a larger sanctuary, the local community government turned down the request to build. The decision was appealed, and it went through a series of court hearings. Each time, the courts came down on the side of the neighborhood, feeling that their one roadway and bridge would be inundated by the traffic caused by a new megachurch.

It was then that Greg Surratt was told of a neighboring business that had closed that had a large empty space with adequate parking. Surratt arranged for the church to acquire the property. They appealed to the governmental authorities, explaining that the church would operate within the existing code and parameters for the building.

The satellite began on a Sunday morning with local leadership directing the praise worship, music, and announcements. The sermon was presented by Surratt by video. From the beginning, visitors came in casual dress because it was not in a church sanctuary but a building that had been a former commercial establishment.

With this model, some complain that the taped sermon is not live preaching. Andy Stanley in North Point Community Church in North Atlanta thought of a unique response to this concern. He was meeting in a large auditorium with over 2,000 people and opened a second worship auditorium in the same facilities for the Sunday morning sermon using a video. Stanley appeared live on one platform for part of the service, then on the next for another part. However, the people did not know until the last minute in which auditorium he would preach live. He found out the people in both auditoriums were engaged in the sermon, whether presented onscreen or live. Stanley noted that even when he was live in an auditorium, some were more engaged with the sermon on the screen than with him live on the stage. It was then that he knew the video venue would work. One note of application: the preacher must be larger onscreen than he is in real life. The large screen demands attention.

Surratt found that this model worked for him too. He preaches live in the main service and uses a video presentation in the satellite location. However, on some occasions he preaches live in a satellite service, showing the video feed in the original building on the island. He found that people got as much out of the taped sermon as they did from the live sermon. From that moment on, the idea of the video venue was off and running.

Today, Seacoast Church has 13 campuses from Savannah, Georgia, to Fayetteville, North Carolina. Many of those campuses offer multiple services so that each weekend there are a total of 29 worship services at Seacoast Church.

Surratt says that you must ask three crucial questions when thinking about starting a multisite church. First, are there people available in the area where you plan to start a satellite church? He tells a church planter to study the demographics of an area to find out if there are people who might come to a satellite campus.

A second question: Is there a need in the community for this type of church? He said this avoids competition with other growing, like-minded churches in a community.

Third question: Will the new campus be located in a growing community? Usually it is new people moving into an area that provide attendance at a start-up campus. It is from these people that the congregation will grow.

Surratt emphasizes the need to find a great location for the new church community because a poor location will stifle the new campus. For Surratt, an ideal auditorium seats a minimum of 300 adults and has space for a children's ministry. It must have parking for 200 cars. Why? To reach a critical mass in today's society, there must be a place for people to park their cars as they attend a church service. There must be at least one or two parking spaces for each person you expect to attend.

Surratt says that the best time to start a new church is in the fall, right after school starts. At that time of year, everything is starting up. Retail sales are gearing up for fall traffic, as well as businesses, the government, and the entire economy.

Next, Surratt says, "Launching a new campus is similar to adding a new worship service to an existing campus. There needs to be a built-in group of people willing to become part of the new worship service in the same building, just as a new location must have a group of people willing to be part of the new campus start-up."

Because Seacoast Church uses video sermons to communicate the Sunday morning message, Surratt feels it's absolutely critical to find a person to be the leader of the new campus. This person must be committed to the lead pastor's preaching and must take responsibility for all other aspects of the new satellite church's ministry. He/she will determine the spiritual atmosphere and direction of the satellite church and how the people will follow the lead of the main church.

The first task of the new leader is to begin building a core team. He will draw from his family and friends and other contacts in the church. Usually there will be people in the initial team sent from the mother church who will be potential leaders for the new campus.

Long before the new campus ever meets, the group should begin meeting on a regular basis for prayer, planning, and vision casting. Surratt also suggests an early meeting called a "vision picnic." People from Seacoast are invited to attend a picnic for the new launch. Invitations should go out to people in the area who have never attended Seacoast as well as to anyone they can reach. The primary aim at a vision picnic is to share the vision of the new church. When people buy into the vision, they will buy into the leadership and make it happen.

Surratt also thinks that it takes about three months of prayer, planning, and hands-on experience for the new campus leader and staff to buy into the values and vision of the new church campus. He goes on to say that this new group is not ready to launch until there are at least 22-30 adults who are meeting on a regular basis to plan and pray.

Once the core group reaches 60-80 they are ready for a new campus launch. That launch will begin on a Sunday, the Lord's Day. When Seacoast Church launches a new campus, Surratt usually attends and makes sure that he meets all the invited guests from the neighborhood and the friends of those from the sending church in attendance.

HISTORY

Some see the multisite church as a continuation of the circuit-riding Methodist preachers during the growth of the early United States Methodist church in the late 1700s and early 1800s.

The circuit-riding preachers were also called "ploughboy preachers" because they were recruited from working on the farm or in a shop to preaching on the weekends. Most were not theologically trained in colleges or seminaries. John Wesley had said he would ordain a man if he had letters (could read and write), numbers (could count), and had the Holy Spirit. To get their sermons, circuit-riding preachers would attend the monthly conference for two or three days to be inspired, taught, and given sermons to preach.

In England, their conferences were led by men such as John Wesley, Charles Wesley, and others who preached from early morning until the evening hour, one sermon after another. The circuit-riding ploughboy preachers would write the sermons down as they heard them. In essence, they would fill up their bucket with biblical content and drink in the power of the Holy Spirit. The bucket of sermons was then poured out, or delivered in power when re-preached.

The circuit rider covered one or more counties on his horse, establishing 30 to 40 congregations, preaching the same sermon in all his churches. The phrase "shouting Methodists" is often used to describe the early Methodist preachers. As they traveled the countryside, they shouted praise to the Lord, sang lustily the songs of Zion, and declared the Gospel to everyone in earshot. Approximately every five miles, the circuit rider gathered people into a tavern, stable, barn, or large home to deliver the sermon he had heard in conference. The power he felt when he heard the sermons was poured out onto the new congregation. Circuit riders may have preached once or twice a day and repeated the same sermon day after day. The following month, he would preach a new sermon or new series of sermons. With time, these small gatherings became churches. Land was purchased, and buildings were built. Traveling historic roads in the United States, one can see a Methodist church about every five miles from one county seat to another.

The Methodists called their many churches a "circuit," each church hearing the same sermon from the same preacher. These sermons developed the same vision in all the churches. Limited by constraints of time and geography, these circuits were much like the multisite churches being built today. As in the Methodist circuits of the 1800s, in today's multisite churches different tools and techniques are used to bring congregations together and the same *vision* and *values* are communicated.

One of the advantages of a multisite church is that space is never a limitation. Many single-site churches grow into the size of their physical structure and never grow any larger than it. But when a second or third site is added, they don't have to deal with the limitation of parking, Sunday school space, etc. The only thing that limits a multisite church is its vision.

MULTISITE CHURCHES IN SCRIPTURE

Technically, the local church is made up of two entities, that is, cells and celebration. Celebration is when people come together to celebrate God by worship, praise, and exhortation, plus preaching and teaching the Word of God. Today, this is called the "worship service." Cells are small groups of people who express their faith but do it in their small, relational interaction. We know these cells today as Sunday school classes, home groups, or Bible studies.

Notice this division in Scripture: *"daily in the temple (celebration), and in every house (cell group), they ceased not to preach (celebration activity), and teach (cell activity), the Word of God"* (Acts 5:42 ELT).

Therefore, in the early church, cells in homes were for teaching, explanation, relationship, involvement, and accountability. Celebration in the temple was for motivation; declaration of the Word of God; expression of passion, testimony, and worship.

There seems to be a designation of more than one house church or different church entities in certain cities where the Gospel had been established. When Paul writes the Book of Romans, he addresses it *"to all that be in Rome, beloved of God..."* (Rom. 1:7 KJV). As far as Paul was concerned, this represents all the people in the church in Rome. Note he greets the Christians that met in the home of Priscilla and Aquila (see Rom. 16:3-5). Later he greets the household of Aristobulus, suggesting another church was in their house (see Rom. 16:10). He does the same when he says, *"Greet them that be of the household of Narcissus, which are in the Lord"* (Rom. 16:11 KJV). Then Paul makes a unique designation, saluting *"the churches of Christ"* (Rom. 16:16 KJV). This description may refer to Jewish churches because Jews were looking for the Messiah. They would have chosen the title "Christ" as a reflection of the Jewish orientation.

To make sure Paul didn't divide the church in Rome, he exhorts, *"Keep your eyes on those who cause dissentions and hindrances contrary to the teachings which you receive"* (Rom. 16:17 ELT). Paul recognized the cultural differences but did not let them divide the group; rather, he kept them united around the Person of Christ. As he says, *"In this new life, it doesn't matter if you are a Jew or a Gentile, circumcised or uncircumcised, barbaric, uncivilized, slave, or free. Christ is all that matters, and He lives in all of us"* (Col. 3:11 NLT).

WAS THE EPHESIAN CHURCH A MULTISITE ONE?

When Paul went to Ephesus, he *"entered the synagogue and reasoned with the Jews"* (Acts 18:19). Apparently, some responded positively to Paul's message, because the Bible says that *"they asked him to stay a longer time with them…"* (Acts 18:20). He stayed there a year and a half, remaining in that city longer than any other place up to that time. After ministering in the synagogue for about three months, some believed *"reasoning and persuading concerning the things of the kingdom of God"* (Acts 19:8). But others rejected it. The message of Paul became a center of controversy so the church was moved to the school of Tyrannus. The Greek word scholé referred to a lecture hall.

We're not sure what this building was when the church met there. It could have been named for a Jewish rabbi named Tyrannus, who was sympathetic to Paul. It could have been a public hall named after the original owner. Still others believed it was a school of a Sophist. But Paul continued that ministry for two years, *"so that all who dwelt in Asia heard the word of the Lord Jesus, both Jews and Greeks"* (Acts 19:10). From this one mother church, Paul evangelized the surrounding areas, planting churches. Was this the first multisite church? Did each church see themselves as completely independent and unaffiliated with the mother church? Or, was there a network connection such as what is found in multisite churches?

Those churches around Ephesus are those mentioned in Revelation: Smyrna, Pergamos, Thyatira, Sardis, Philadelphia, and Laodicea (see Rev. 1:11). Ephesus was the seventh. Colossae was in that area but was not involved in the seven churches of Revelation. However, this was the city to whom the Book of Colossians was written. Also, Paul's letter to Philemon was written to him as a church leader in Colossae.

SECOND-GENERATION LEADERS

Not only was it important to plant new churches, but it was also important to develop programs to teach potential members of that church so they could become leaders of new churches. They had to learn character, biblical content, and effective ministry to carry on the work of the church.

The success of every new church plant was tied to the effectiveness of its training. Therefore, when describing a multisite church, give attention to developing and teaching a team who will start another new church and ultimately be responsible for the multiplication of churches.

Multiplication grows out of vision. When beginning a new church plant, the members must have a vision for planting another church. They should begin praying, planting, and working toward another church plant after theirs is successfully planted.

Training the second generation was explained by Paul: *"And the things that you have heard from me among many witnesses, commit these to faithful men who will be able to teach others also"* (2 Tim. 2:2). Because Paul was committed to preaching the Gospel in every city, he was committed to training others to carry on church planting.

So, Paul gathered young believers around him who could first learn from him as he did ministry. Then they would do ministry with him. And in the process, he taught them how to do ministry so they were enabled to carry on the ministry after he was gone.

When the men Paul trained were mature enough, he could launch them out into ministry on their own. And as a result, they would plant their own church to do their own ministry.

The first generation was Paul, the second generation was Timothy, the third generation were faithful men, but it didn't stop there. They should be willing and able to teach others also (see 2 Tim 2:2b). Thus, Paul needed to set in motion leadership development as an unending chain for church multiplication. Developing natural and spiritual abilities are important for church planting. Paul looked for one thing that was even more important: "*faithful men*" (2 Tim. 2:2). Faithfulness was the most important virtue in church planting.

The key to successful church planting is relationship between the first and second generation, between Paul and Timothy. Anyone can have physical children, but it takes spiritual commitment and passion to communicate your inward *values* and *vision* to the next generation.

Again, look at that verse in Second Timothy. Timothy *heard*; then he was to *teach* others. Finally, notice the word *communicate*—the lessons must be passed on to the fourth generation.

Why does so much church planting fail? Many people feel that Bible facts or content are the most important things to communicate. But Bible knowledge alone is not the key. Timothy had to learn how to receive knowledge, skills, passions, and results. Then he had to pass it on to the third generation. To make sure it didn't die with them, all he learned had to be passed on to the fourth generation.

ADVANTAGES OF MULTISITE CHURCHES

One of the great advantages of a multisite church is that it brings together some of the best aspects of both the large mother church and the new small church being started.

It's not just increasing the total number of seats available, nor is it adding an additional service time, another place, or more space. It has everything to do with faith and passion. If you are passionate about your faith in Jesus Christ, you want to pass that passion on to others in as many different ways as possible.

Multisite churches overcome geographic barriers after a church's facilities are landlocked or tightly zoned. Multisite church planning can jump from one neighborhood to another, from the city to the county, and can cross state lines and national boundaries.

Multisite churches will tap into unused talent and give opportunities for individuals to develop new energies and abilities to serve the Lord. This means they are developing more spiritual gifts than they've had before.

When you start a new multisite campus, volunteers are mobilized to get involved and make it happen. A multisite campus never happens because of organization and administration alone. It always has to do with opportunity and willingness to serve.

Also, a multisite church increases the options of worship styles. As a church moves from one neighborhood to another, it may transition from one culture to a different one. That may mean different music expressions in terms of volume, tone, and value.

Therefore, a multisite church accelerates a climate for diversity. Because it can move from one culture to another, it can become more creative and innovative in ministry styles and methods. That involves everything from announcements, to music, to personal relationships.

And another thing: a new multisite church will attract friends, relatives, and neighbors from the core people of the new campus. Whereas some might have been unwilling to travel a great distance to the original church location, they may be willing to attend or be involved in a church closer to their home. Perhaps they will get involved because the new campus has incorporated their friends into its ministry.

Finally, a multisite church can extend itself into small cultural niches that may not otherwise be reached for the Gospel. They can start services in hospital wards, retirement homes, office complexes, or even private homes. These cells can become a part of a larger church and receive the strength of the greater church, whereas ministry done in a hospital ward or retirement home without attachment to a local church may just be another Christian meeting without permanence or stability.

WEAKNESSES OR QUESTIONS ABOUT MULTISITE CHURCHES

While there are many advantages to multisite churches, there are some questions that must be faced. In a culture that is increasingly unchurched, where more people have no religious memory, will a better and more convenient multisite church make a difference? Technically, the site does not make the difference. It is the people at the site, their relationship to the new community, and the testimony they have for Jesus Christ that will make all the difference in the world.

Over a period of time there could be the issue of diminishing influence of "hero image" in the large single church. All leaders ultimately reach their plateau. But in a multisite church, leaders and/or dominant personalities that created the multisite church in the first place are not the total picture. New leaders are growing and developing, and they can become influential as role models.

What happens when the original pioneer dies or moves on? Will the second and third generation be able to carry on as effectively as the first generation? Many times the personality of the leader holds the church and its sites together. However, when he is gone, the glue that holds the organization together is not as effective unless the second- or third-generation leader becomes just as strong or stronger.

Another question: Some pastoral ministries in the mother church may be very effective, but can they always be that effective in a campus by another pastor, with another approach? Will it be the same when the pastor of a satellite church prays over the sick (see James 5:14) as it was when the founding pastor prayed? Also, what about watching over the sheep, leading in breaking bread and sharing the cup (see Acts 2:42)? Will those be the same?

And then there's another question that needs to be asked. The ability to hold many churches together depends, many times, on the speaking ability of the senior pastor who is seen on the video tape and/or closed-circuit television. If the next or second pastor doesn't have that same ability, can he keep the flock together? Can he keep people ministering together for the same goal?

Many times the multisite church moves into a new neighborhood and does a better job than the stand-alone church that is already in the community. Is better enough? Is it better simply because it attracts more people? Perhaps the real question to ask is, is either church reproducible? If something can't be reproduced, maybe it has reached its natural limitations. This is also true for a church: when a church can't reproduce itself, its natural limitation has been reached.

Another problem is the perception by many who come from independent, unaffiliated, local churches. They have always thought of the lead pastor as their shepherd and their preacher. Who is the *real* pastor—the multi-campus pastor or the mother church pastor? There are questions that arise when a pastor becomes a bishop to oversee a number of churches or campuses. Some think the unity and nature of the local church is violated by the multisite church, hence why they question its biblical nature.

WHAT CAN WE LEARN FROM MULTISITE CHURCHES?

The multisite church did not grow because a few handfuls of innovative churches were doing it better. Also, it didn't come from a megachurch that just wanted to get bigger and/or reach more. Nor is a multisite church doing what other churches are doing. There are many advantages of the multisite church planting model. First, the multisite church can present the best arguments for both the large and the small church at the same time. All the arguments that a church should be large, reaching out, and saturating a town for Christ are answered by the multisite church. At the same time, the small intimate flock based on relationships is seen in the small church.

The multisite church can overcome economic barriers, geographical barriers, ethnic barriers, and some cultural barriers. It's a way of carrying out the Great Commission, bringing the Gospel to all people, in all places, at all times. Remember, Jesus said, *"Go therefore, and make disciples of all the nations..."* (Matt. 28:19).

The very nature of a multisite church means that it's making greater use of a broader range of spiritual gifts and talents of those who are in the church. It means there must be more ushers, more greeters, more technicians, more musicians—more of everything. When there are more people doing ministry, it's only natural that there are more ministers.

And then, the multisite church may be able to produce more authentic worship because people can worship in the congregation size where they feel more comfortable and when they feel they best express their praise to the Lord.

And don't forget, multisite churches keep local churches local. In a day in which people can drive 50 to 100 miles to a church, why should they do that when a multisite church can send a congregation to them?

And doesn't a multisite church stretch your Kingdom vision? It gives you more Kingdom outreach for the glory of God.

But then again, look at the very nature of the Great Commission. A multisite church produces churches that are reproducing themselves in evangelism and discipleship.

Have we come to a time when the multisite church has become a natural extension of the megachurch phenomena of the 1970s and 1980s? We went through an age when people thought the church was getting bigger and bigger; auditoriums were seating more until they were as big as sports venues. And then Andy Stanley told an audience, "If you believe in the vitality of the megachurch, it is hard to argue against the multisite church."

That brings us to another area of expectation. No matter what we do, or what we create, or where we grow, we always expect to do it bigger and better. So, we step up to the challenge of reaching more, doing more, and being a greater influence in the world through the multisite church.

Then there's a pragmatic issue. Multisite churches simply work. Satellite churches function well because they usually offer only the main ministries of a local church, for example, Sunday worship and small groups, whereas the mother church will usually have the other needed ministries, such as feeding the hungry, clothing the needy, targeting community needs, and providing other age-specific or niche ministries. The mother churches can do it all because they offer small-group intimacy and meet large church expectations.

Finally, consider that when you take a church to where the people are, the outreach of a church diminishes. But the multisite church goes to where new people are located and has unlimited potential. New horizons are established, and boundaries are diminished. Isn't that good?

CHAPTER 8

PLANTING HOUSE CHURCHES

There are many places in the world today where Christianity is grow-ing because *house churches* are being planted.

But as previously noted, perhaps the greatest house church move-ment in the world today is the underground church movement in Communist China. It is estimated to have more than 100 million believers. It represents the resurrected power of the Gospel because like the phoenix, it has arisen from the ashes of destruction.

In the late 1940s, Communist forces defeated the Nationalist forces of General Chiang Kai-shek and began a systematic purge of "Western" Christianity. The government seized all the property and buildings of the Christians, including churches, schools, denomi-national headquarters, dormitories, etc. Church leaders were either martyred or sent into camps or prisons. The outward evidence of Christianity and its ages of ministry vanished almost overnight.

In September 1950, my missions teacher at Columbia Bible Col-lege was Arthur Glasser, who represented China Inland Missions.

The devastating stories he told left me bewildered. I wanted to cry out, "Why, God?"

Sixty years later, I was huddled in the back of a restaurant in Shanghai, China, listening to 22 leaders from house churches telling me one thrilling testimony after another of the explosion of the underground church in China. Each of the 22 leaders supervised a system of house churches, some a dozen churches, others as many as 200 house churches. They told how the number of churches grew with each wave of persecution. One leader testified, "God allowed the Communists to wipe out the influence of Western Christianity so we could have a pure Chinese church. We do not have buildings, headquarters, schools, classrooms, dormitories, or offices. All we have is people and church and the power of the Gospel."[1]

The growth and strength of the Chinese house church movement is not measured by outward things that define Western Christianity but by the power of God and the church's inner purpose and nature. Western Christianity draws strength from its cathedrals, sanctuaries, and unique structures built throughout cities. Many times these are built in prominent places to attract people to its faith. Historic Western church landmarks tell of Christianity's glorious past, but the Chinese house church movement is not focused on buildings or structures.

Western Christianity has an abundance of programs to instruct, evangelize, and serve humanitarian needs. Its programs rally its members to a cause, then educate them, equip them and direct them to great crusades. But Chinese Christianity operates out of simplistic New Testament purposes, not programs.

Western Christianity is led by its educated, equipped, and dedicated leaders. Attached to most denominations are schools of higher education or seminaries. To be a Western leader, a young man or woman must obtain college and seminary training, embrace ordination standards, and measure up to some of the highest academic standards in the world. Their schools are academic based and accredited by secular and governmental agencies. But have educational standards alone made Western Christianity strong? The Chinese house church is driven by lay leaders who are equipped through ministry-based and church-based programs that have no accreditation recognition.

Western Christianity is known by its huge denominational organizations that drive their missionary outreach. The most popular of these might be the Episcopal, Presbyterian, Methodist, and Baptist denominations, and among these are growing evangelical groups such as the Pentecostals and the Nazarenes. The house church of China is not defined by denominational tribes, although some divisions exist in China. These Chinese divisions inform outside observers who they are and what they are doing. For the most part, the "church distinctions" in China do not serve or advance churches; they exist to identify churches.

THE HOUSE CHURCH

A house is just a structure where people live, but it becomes a home when it's defined by the family who lives there, and it gains meaning by how they live. A house church can be a two-bedroom apartment on the thirty-ninth floor of a modern high-rise in Seoul, Korea. A church meets in their apartment, and the church is organized similar to how a family gets things done. The husband and wife who live in the apartment define their life by their intimate relationship with each other. The house church also defines itself by the same type of loving relationship.

A family with a rice farm in Thailand defines their home by the tasks of father, mother, and children. They put food on the table and care for their basic necessities. Their focus is planting rice, tending to the young plants, and feverishly harvesting them. The church that meets in their home is defined by the way it feeds on the Word of God and carries out the ministry of Jesus Christ.

Another home is defined by the education of its children. Both father and mother instruct children in their basic necessities. Older children also help instruct the young to live in a happy and healthy manner. Some house churches are focused primarily on training and preparing their members to live for Christ.

What makes a house church a house church? It is more than using a church in a house. A home church is defined by the activities that go on there. Don't think of a church as four walls, a floor, and roof. A church is more than a dwelling place or a meeting place protected from the elements. The nature of a church is defined by what it is and what it does. A church is defined by its life within the four walls, not by the structure in which it meets.

Remember, the church is Jesus Christ, and the Bible calls a church His body (see Eph. 1:22-23). So, when people gather together with Jesus in His presence, how do they do it? In many ways.

Some home churches are worshiping churches. Many people attend a house church because they realize that you cannot be in the presence of God without recognizing His nature and glorifying Him. Remember, worship is giving the worth to God that belongs to Him. When God shows up, the true worshiper gives Him the worth due to Him.

Some home churches are defined by their labor and ministry. Members come together to pray for lost friends and relatives. They come together to plan evangelism and how they will deliver the message of Jesus. Thus, a home church is defined by the evangelistic ministry of each member as they serve the Lord together.

Other house churches are defined by their passionate educational endeavors, and they give themselves to discipling new believers in their faith. They teach Christian character to one another and to their young. Their educational ministry defines their church.

Still other house churches resemble perpetual Bible study class. Members open the Scriptures to share what they have learned or ask questions to learn what they don't know. The house church is an educational body where they come together to know Christ and prepare themselves to make Him known.

THE EARLY CHURCH WAS A HOUSE MOVEMENT

The Jewish culture was defined by three strong sociological entities: the home, the synagogue, and the temple. The home was the basic unit of society and determined the life and direction of the way Jews lived their faith. The synagogue was where Jewish families came together to worship God, reinforce their faith to one another, and communicate their faith to their young ones. The temple was the foundation of Jewish culture. It was the location where God dwelt, and when Jews entered it, they felt they were entering God's presence. True, Jews believed God was omniscient, meaning God was present everywhere. Also, God had an indwelling presence in each Jewish believer. But the localized presence of God was manifested in the temple, and it was there that the Jews came to worship and celebrate their faith in Him.

The early house church incorporated these three entities. First, they met in house churches that became the backbone of Christianity. The biological family unit became the foundation of Christianity; the husband and wife prayed together, worked together, and reproduced the life of Christ in their children. So it was only natural that the church should meet in homes where their spiritual life was celebrated and reproduced in their young.

Second, early Christians went to the synagogue because that was a place of teaching/learning. It was there that they expressed their faith to other Jews and therefore a place where early Christians witnessed their faith in Jesus Christ to their unsaved friends. Every time Paul went to a new city, he went to the local synagogue.

Third, the Jewish Christians went to the temple because God was there. They worshiped God in the temple, celebrated His presence, enjoyed the manifestations of His goodness, and met with other believers there. *"Every day, in the Temple and from house to house, they continued to teach and preach this message: 'Jesus is the Messiah'"* (Acts 5:42 NLT).

No place in the world is the house church more prevalent today than in Mainland China. Churches registered with the government are located mostly in cities, but house churches are everywhere—cities, small towns, and rural areas. But no one knows where they are located. What a contrast to American Christianity, where churches are located on the corners of many streets and everyone knows the church by its steeple and/or the uniqueness of its structure. But the China house church doesn't advertise or use any type of publicity—hence why it's referred to as the "underground church"—and yet it has become one of the most powerful Christian movements in the world.

Unofficially, there is estimated to be more than 130 million believers in China today. The official Three-Self Church in China is recognized by the government and has a registration of approximation 23.5 million believers. The Three-Self Church is divided by denominations recognized by Western Christianity and has higher education support for the clergy. China has over 1.5 billion people with more than 100 million believers meeting in house churches in homes, apartments, restaurants, and other places.

Observers suggest that there was no underground church in 1949 when the Communists took over the government of China. Today, Christianity has exploded in China so that perhaps one-tenth of the population identifies with Jesus Christ. That's astounding considering the Communist government is unfriendly to Christianity.

Note the contrast to America, where Christianity is coddled by the government and recognized as a major contributor to its culture. America is described as having a Protestant-Puritan ethnic. But American Christianity is weak and does not have the influence it once had. Some have likened American Christianity to senior citizens living in a retirement home, where inhabitants dream of a past life well spent; but like old folks in the rest home, they have no viable future.

PERSECUTION—ITS GREATEST BLESSING

I spoke to 22 leaders of underground churches in China when I was in Shanghai in 2008. We met on a Friday evening in a darkened restaurant, and when I heard a stranger enter the restaurant, my first reaction was to think that the police had come to spy on us or arrest us.

Each of the 22 people had a network of house churches to which they gave supervision and direction. One told about people riding their bicycles to church and how when too many bicycles appeared in an apartment building, the police became suspicious and disrupted the assembly. When the police located the church in an apartment, the owner's lease was cancelled and they lost the money they had put into it.

When this happened, the church immediately was divided into three smaller churches, meeting at three different sections of the city. How could they do that? Because all members are expected to minister the Word of God at each meeting.

As soon as a new believer is welcomed into a house church, they understand it is their duty to study the Scriptures before the next house meeting. They study it carefully and come prepared to share what they have learned. All adults are expected to share, pray, and lead in worship, singing, and group activities.

The house church's division into three churches was not a challenge of leadership. The adults in each of the house churches carried on their leadership activities. They continued to share, pray together, and lead together. What does this mean? Persecution grew this church.

The house church in China grows without buildings, organized structure, programs, denominational support, or influence from the West. Their influence and motivation comes from God, who speaks directly to each person and guides the church through each leader.

WHAT IS A HOUSE CHURCH?

A house church describes an independent assembly of believers who gather in homes to carry out ministry functions described in the New Testament. Most house churches are smaller than the traditional institutional church. They meet in a home just as a physical family finds an appropriate structure to gather to carry out its functions.

House churches grow through relationship evangelism. For the most part, they do not have programs or methods of evangelistic outreach such as Evangelism Explosion, the Four Spiritual Laws, or the Roman Road of Salvation. As one person connects to a friend or family, they relate their faith to that person and encourage them to become a part of their faith.

Many people believe that Jesus intended the church to be in a home. They look at the absence of church buildings in the New Testament and ask why we have resorted to church buildings today.

The house church may be the same size as the home cell, but the two have different identities. House churches are independently organized and indigenously operated. A home cell group is only part of a larger church's ministry. A home cell group and a house church may look similar in their functions, but the home cell group is connected to a larger fellowship whereas a house church is not.

The house church is usually independent organizationally from other church groups, yet they function interdependently with other groups of like nature and practice. They fellowship together and at times minister together.

Parallels can be drawn between people becoming part of a house church and becoming a part of a new family. In a house church, there is usually no official activity of placing a new name on the church roll or voting them into church membership. Similar to a biological family, where children become a part of the family because they are born physically to the father and mother, new Christians become a part of the church family in a house church because they are born again through the ministry of its members.

Neil Cole advances the idea in his book *Organic Church* that "the world is interested in Jesus and what He is doing in the world, but they're not so much interested in His bride. Therefore, people are reluctant to attend church, give excuses for attendance, and find reasons not to be there on a Sunday."[2] Cole suggests that when the world resists being in fellowship with the Bride of Christ, there is something wrong with the bride. He contends that when Christian life becomes a facility-based ministry rather than a person-based ministry, it loses family relationships.

Perhaps the problem is that the church has suffered from the physical successes of its excesses. Sometimes what happens is that when a house church is growing, it needs larger facilities that are more conducive to its ministry and purpose. Therefore, it builds a place of worship where people can sit and worship, gather in ministry, and from that location go out into the world to serve Jesus Christ. But as the church facilities grow larger and the building becomes more extensive and expensive, the success of its ministry demands the continuance of its ministry. The church becomes captive to its own success and is controlled by its structure.

SPIRITUAL PRACTICES OF HOUSE CHURCHES

A house church is defined by participation of all the members of the church body. Approximately 93 percent of the members lead out in spoken prayer during their meetings, and 90 percent will read from the Bible. About 87 percent will spend time sharing their personal needs and experiences, for example, giving testimonies during group meetings.

Eating becomes important in a house church, and 85 percent of the time is spent in eating and fellowshipping together. Usually around 83 percent of the people get involved in the discussion of a teaching topic.

House churches spend about 70 percent of their time with music or singing, followed by a word from the Scriptures and/or a special word delivered to them.

Not all house churches take an offering. Sometimes the offering is taken in an informal way, with someone passing money to a certain person for a specific topic and/or need. However, about half the house churches take a collection on a regular basis and from those funds pay for special needs and projects.

In addition, not all house churches serve communion. About half of them will serve communion on a given Sunday. A few will serve communion once a month, and some serve communion on a quarterly basis. And a very few will have communion once or twice a year, usually at Christmas and Easter.

THE HOME, THE PRIMARY PLACE OF INFLUENCE

Throughout Scripture, the home is the primary place of influence for individuals, and the house church is the primary place that influences the growth and health of individual believers. When Joshua said, *"...But as for me and my house, we will serve the Lord"* (Josh. 24:15), he was reflecting the strength that comes from family unity.

The Jews recognized that God built the family through individual members: *"Unless the Lord builds the house, they labor in vain who build it..."* (Ps. 127:1).

The early church not only ate their physical meals together; they also ate communion meals in common with other believers, *"...breaking bread from house to house..."* (Acts 2:46).

However, it was more than communion that was shared. Before and after the service, the ministry of teaching continued: *"daily in the temple, and in every house, they did not cease teaching and preaching Jesus as the Christ"* (Acts 5:42).

Because the home was the focus of Christianity, when Saul began persecuting the church, trying to get rid of it, he attacked families and the house church. The Bible speaks of *"Saul...entering every house..."* (Acts 8:3).

Because the home was so influential, Paul told the Philippian jailer, *"Believe on the Lord Jesus Christ, and you will be saved, you and your household"* (Acts 16:31). That's why Paul used house teaching to communicate Christianity, *"publicly and from house to house"* (Acts 20:20). When Paul began to write to the churches, he wrote to the church in Corinth, in the *"house of Chloe"* (1 Cor. 1:11 ELT). Also, he notes that there was a church in *"the household of Stephanas"* (1 Cor. 16:15). On another occasion, Paul instructs, *"Greet the brethren who are in Laodicea, and Nymphas and the church that is in his house"* (Col.

4:15). When Paul wrote to Philemon, he also sent greetings, *"to the beloved Apphia, Archippus our fellow soldier, and to the church in your house"* (Philem. 1:2).

Because the church was so important and a means of fellowship, it was also a means of discipline. When someone was put out of the church, they were not allowed to attend the house meeting. As the Bible says, *"...do not receive him into your house..."* (2 John 10).

When Paul wrote to the church of Rome, because there was probably more than one house church in Rome he addresses himself *"to all who are in Rome...beloved of God, called to be saints..."* (Rom. 1:7). He didn't address this letter to one church, as other letters were written to the church in Corinth and Thessalonica (see 1 Cor. 1:2; 1 Thess. 1:1). However, because there were many house churches in the city of Rome, he wrote to believers in Rome. Then Paul specifically directed his attention to one house church: *"Greet Priscilla and Aquila...who risked their own necks.... Likewise greet the church that is in their house..."* (Rom. 16:3-5). Perhaps there was one house church in Rome that was made up of primarily Jewish believers. So he writes, *"...The churches of Christ greet you"* (Rom. 16:16). Because the word *Christ* is the word *Messiah*, this designation suggests Jewish fulfillment. These churches were identified by the Jewish name Messiah.

Paul made sure that all the churches in Rome were unified; he didn't want to divide them. *"I urge you, brethren, note those who cause divisions and offenses, contrary to the doctrine which you learned, and avoid them"* (Rom. 16:17). The principle here was to recognize cultural differences but not to let them divide the church of Jesus Christ. There is unity around the Person of Jesus. Remember: Jesus attracts, but doctrine sometimes divides.

Paul said, *"In this new life, it doesn't matter if you are a Jew or a Gentile, circumcised or uncircumcised, barbaric, uncivilized, slave, or free. Christ is all that matters, and he lives in all of us"* (Col. 3:11 NLT).

ADVANTAGES OF THE HOUSE CHURCH

1. *The house church is a community.* The very nature of a house church is that people come into a church family to experience a face-to-face relationship with others in *koinonia*, or fellowship. Just as a physical family lives together, so a spiritual house church family lives their Christian life together with others, before others, and for others.

Much of Western Christianity is identified with organizations, programs, and the institutional nature of the church. It has become one of the social institutions of society. But many Christians leave the institutional church because they desire the close fellowship of a house church. They are looking for deeper spiritual intimacy with other believers. Many American Christians could be called "disenfranchised Christians" because they have their name on a roll and call a physical structure their church home—but they never go home.

A house church fulfills a person's expectations of family. They call each other sister and brother, and they worship together. When they talk about their house church, they describe an intimacy and interrelatedness of a unified body as it fellowships together and works together for the glory of God.

2. *House churches are communities of conviction.* When someone joins a typical Western church, they usually have to affirm their faith through an external identity, for example, the doctrinal statement or covenant of the local church. They enter through baptism, either by sprinkling or by immersion, after they have learned doctrine and/or the expectations of the new Christian life. Once they meet these qualifications and are voted into fellowship, they become part of a local church.

However, becoming a part of a house church is an interactive identity where they become a part of a new house church by living in a house church, worshiping in a house church, and sharing their Christian life in their house church.

By living in the house church, they open themselves up to life-changing experiences of the others in the house church. They become one with the other house church people, and as a result, they have a greater level of intimacy than people usually experience in a building-based church ministry.

Most house churches are not held together by written principles that people know and learn; rather, they learn to live as Christians by living like Christians who are members of that house church.

Very seldom is there a covenant and/or pledge that is necessary to join a house church. This is used by institution-based churches. But people in a house church make a deeper commitment to the values and experiences of other Christians in their fellowship. And by living as other Christians live, they become part of the house church family.

3. *House churches are learning communities.* Those who join a house church find a sense of family or community oneness not experienced in the traditional Western church. Just as a family must instruct its members on how to live in the family, relate in the family, and prepare for life outside the family, the same is true for a house church family. The nature of a house church community is to share its experiences with all new members and then reciprocate by blessing and being blessed. Given the isolated nature of most individuals, those joining a house church open up their lives to change, growth, and maturity.

Obviously, not everyone has the same experience when they come into a house church. They all begin at the same place: they meet Jesus Christ, and they are born again; and they begin from that experience. They must understand the experiences that happen to them, understand what God has done for them, and understand their relationship to other members in the new house community.

4. *House churches are faith formation communities.* Often Western Christianity teaches Christianity in a classroom setting, but in a house church, you learn Christianity from daily experiences and relationships. Obviously, there is a doctrinal statement of faith that people know, believe, and want to practice. In a house church, there is not a classroom environment where a teacher attempts to communicate a doctrinal statement and get people to know, memorize, and repeat the statement.

In the New Testament, faith is both a noun and a verb. As a noun, it is a reference to the doctrinal statement of faith, that is, a statement to be internalized and memorized. However, faith is also a verb suggesting action, life, or experiences. Faith is trusting Jesus, obeying Jesus, and following Jesus.

Most house churches do not vote in believers when they join, nor do they sign a doctrinal statement of faith. Rather, new believers learn faith and doctrine through informal relationships, asking questions, listening to sermons, and/or interacting with other believers.

Members of the house church learn faith (the noun) by exercising faith (the verb) and living for Jesus Christ based on how they have seen others do the same.

Both living faith and doctrinal faith are important and necessary. However, which comes first? In most Western Christianity churches, doctrinal faith comes first. However, in house churches, living faith comes first; people must know the Person of Jesus Christ, live for Him, and reflect their faith in obedience to Him.

House church members react to the Word of God by learning faith. Remember, *"faith comes by hearing, and hearing by the Word of God"* (Rom. 10:17). So, a new believer gains faith by interacting with God's Word, both as he understands it and as he sees it lived in the lives of other people. When a new believer attempts to live the same way as other believers, they follow Jesus Christ and progress in their faith.

5. *House churches are value formation communities.* As the house church community becomes important to new members, the way that people live and the values they express are slowly acquired by new members, who begin to live out what they have learned. New believers find themselves aligning with other believers in the group when they hear and see Christianity modeled and they understand what is required of them. Then they begin to value time, purity, and "Jesus first." They begin to acquire the values of Christianity. The values of purity, integrity, and obedience to God's Word are highly prized. These are best communicated in relationships.

All these value formation activities create a new self-identity for the new believer. He must realize, "I am a follower of Jesus Christ." That's much more important than saying, "I am a Baptist, or a Presbyterian, or a Pentecostal."

6. *House churches are mentoring agents.* Usually, there are no courses for new believers in a house church; they begin living for God when they are born again by praying, sharing, and worshiping together. The values of Christianity and the attitudes toward worship are assimilated through observation and nonverbal experiences, usually through a one-on-one relationship.

Mentoring relationships are usually need driven rather than driven by a study guide and/or a course of study.

As new believers are accepted for who they are, they soon feel the pressure to assume the values and attitudes of the others in the house church. They no longer can live as they did before they were Christians. They bottle up for themselves the new life they see in other believers and become like them. This is nondirective mentoring, but it is extremely effective. There is usually not one individual mentor in a local church; it's usually the total of the house church family mentoring all new believers as they come into their fellowship.

7. *House churches are belonging communities.* A house church offers a network of relationships for the new believer. Believers are accepted for what they have done: they received Jesus Christ as their Savior, and they profess new life in Him. Immediately, they are accepted into the family as equal in relationship but not yet fully matured in experience. The new house church community becomes a powerful force to influence the lives of new believers. The very nature of how a house church worships and experiences the presence of God influences the believers to follow their example. Therefore, it becomes a shared faith, a shared experience, and a shared love.

8. *House churches give self-identity to its members.* When a new believer gives himself to a house community, it doesn't mean he loses his self-identity or a sense of self-belonging. They still have other loyalties outside the house church, and they will identify with other groups outside the church. But their identity in Christ is new, and their relationship to the house church is new.

When a new believer comes into a house church, it doesn't mean that all the people in the house church always believe what every other believer believes. They live in the arena of expectations. Because regeneration influences the central drive of a person's life, their new experiences begin to grow. They form a new identity in Christ. They see, "I am now a Jesus follower."

9. *House church communities encourage hospitality.* Each member of a house church will serve another, respect one another, and as in Scripture, love one another. This means they accept the uniqueness of other people within their community but always respect the freedom of the community to be who they are, while growing together in maturity to Jesus Christ.

As a result, house church communities do little to formally indoctrinate new members into their creed, nor do they demand agreement with their confessional statement of faith in order to become part of the church. Relationship in the new community is the great "glue" that bonds people together, rather than having the doctrinal statement or a vote for membership as the "glue."

SIX MAJOR CATEGORIES OF ORGANIC HOUSE CHURCHES

Many people join house churches to be separate from the institution-focused church, especially in Western Christianity, where there are so many institutional churches. They join house churches to be together with others of like mind and like faith.

In the United States, there are three movements surrounding the home: homeschooling, home birth, and home churches. Individuals get involved in any one of these three functions because they want to be separate from the normal or traditional way of doing things.

Anti-establishment house churches. Sometimes people go into house churches because they have disdain for the traditional church and its practices. They see hypocrisy and shallow Christianity there. Many times, their worship is traditional or superficial, not focused on the end of worship, Jesus Christ Himself. The idea of a formal organizational structure, buildings, and hierarchical authority are an anathema to them. They want to go back to the pure nature of the church that is nothing but Jesus and His relationship to His people. Therefore, they reject the institutional church, its property, programmatic structure, organizations, and/or formalized doctrine.

Deeper understanding. Some attend a house church because they want a deeper understanding of the Word of God and/or more intimacy with God. They read deeper life books and desire a life of victory and/or abiding in God. They see that walking with Jesus is much deeper than the Christianity of the organized church. So, they thrive on information, testimonies, multiple readings of Scripture, group prayers, sharing the spoken Word, and participating together in communion, fellowship, and projects.

Exposition-driven sermons. Many times, people come together in a home church because of their desire to study the Bible in depth. Many of the Plymouth Brethren in the 1800s assembled together because of their interpretation of the Scriptures through a dispensational, pre-tribulation view of the rapture and pre-millennial point of view. The Anabaptists in the 1500s came together for their unique view of believers' baptism. They wanted a personal identification with baptism that was different from the state Protestant church's alignment of church membership with national citizenship.

Spontaneous house churches. Some house churches are not just reacting against Western Christianity or formal churches or any organizational trend of Christianity. They spring up out of a pure need to study the Scriptures, to follow Jesus Christ in their integrity, and to band together for worship and fellowship. These groups usually give the traditional church a secondary role in their life, and their individual walk with Christ and interpretation of Scripture become the guiding principles of their Christian life. Usually, a spontaneous house church is motivated by mature believers, or those who want more intimacy with Jesus Christ. This group is not typically associated with a strong evangelism passion or carrying out the Great Commission.

WEAKNESSES OF THE HOUSE CHURCH MOVEMENT

There are many strengths in the house church movement, but there are also associated weaknesses that are listed below.

Lack of organization. A survey shows that the average house church in the United States lasts approximately 22 months. Does that say something about the character and purpose of the people in the house church, or does it say something about its lack of organization that keeps it going or a lack of perpetuity of purpose? In opposition, Western Christianity features organized churches to carry out the purpose of the church. However, some traditional churches continue to exist even when confused and lacking vision.

Some traditional churches not only have lost their purpose, they have even lost their desire to find a purpose and a reason why they exist. Their ability to carry on tells us that a well-organized church will exist when an unorganized house church will fold up. Therefore, both the strengths and weaknesses of organized churches are arguments against the house church movement. Basically, a group of Christians need both organization and purpose to guarantee its perpetuity.

Potential lack of faith to carry out and implement the purposes of New Testament Christianity. If God was sincere when He gave the Great Commission to evangelize, then some house churches that exist for fellowship, Bible study, and maturity of the believers are not serious about carrying out the purpose of God. The lack of purpose in some house churches reveals their weakness and argues against the very nature of how they do things. Should the leaders of a house church really believe the commands of Jesus Christ they not only would give diligence to obey, but would also follow the natural inclination by developing strategies, programs, and plans to carry out His commands and obey His dictates.

Lack of a doctrinal statement. The house church is committed to Bible study, and the strength of their belief leads to continual growth in the Bible and application of the Scripture to the lives of members. But when a group depends on a doctrinal statement for continuity, the group may fluctuate. When their understanding, comprehension, and/or application wavers, the group wavers. But when a group writes their doctrinal faith in objective statements and commits themselves to know it, believe it, practice it, and defend it, then that group has an objective standard to measure their growth and ministry. Without an objective standard, people are left to their own internal desires and study, which changes because human nature is not perfect and, many times, follows the dictates of its selfish nature.

The lack of a doctrinal statement can cause the house church to drift from its early love of Christianity. But an objective statement and set of standards will direct the human heart back again and again to the truth of God. Commitment and objective standards will keep a church in line and in faith.

4. *Lack of objectives and/or goals of ministry.* When a believer fellowships with others, they grow in that relationship. But that growth must have an objective basis or target. Without standards, individual faith may or may not motivate actions. When the group has objective purposes and measurements, each individual will be motivated to continual action.

Every church should plant another church, just as every Christian must win another person to Jesus Christ. When this is not being done, it's the duty of the pastor/leader to motivate the church to return to its objective purpose to carry out the Great Commission. But the lack of commitment to the Great Commission will eventually weaken a local house church and cause its demise.

5. *Lack of written standards for life and ministry.* When the standards for Christian growth are measured by the Word of God, then believers are motivated to grow and do more for God. However, Christians should not have their eyes on growth standards or another

believer, but on Jesus Christ. Objective standards in the Word of God will measure growth and motivate believers to continued growth.

6. *Lack of standards in church ordinances.* The church has two ordinances. The first is baptism for entrance into the Body of Christ. A believer must realize that baptism is more than a love commitment to Christ or a personal desire to please Christ; baptism fulfills a believer's commitment to be obedient to Jesus Christ. Baptism introduces the new believer into fellowship with other believers. When a house church doesn't make baptism mandatory, it begins to weaken itself. But written standards about baptism bond a church together to carry out the commands of the Great Commission.

The same could be said about communion. Communion should be offered on a regular basis—*"when you come together"* (1 Cor. 11:20). Whether that is daily, weekly, monthly, or annually is not clear in Scripture. The mandate is for a regular basis. Why? So that believers will have a regular checkup on their obedience and growth.

When the New Testament commands, "Eat together" and "All of you drink," it is a command to partake together. So, when Christians don't partake of the Lord's Table on a regular basis, the Christian, as well as the local church, is weakened.

7. *Lack of communication about obligations of individuals to corporate ecclesia.* Many attend the house church because of personal enrichment and/or other personal benefits that result from fellowshipping with others and studying the Word of God together. This is good! However, the Bible gives believers an obligation to attend services on a regular basis in worship, fellowship, offerings, and service. The house church depends on its members to obey according to the dictates of their heart. But their nature can become their standard and the basis for their obedience. When they find reasons in their heart not to attend, participate, or give financially, they weaken

their faith, and then the church becomes weak. However, in institutional churches, standards of participation and/or obligations keep local churches strong.

CONCLUSION

A house church is one of the first ways the church was described in the New Testament. *"So continuing daily with one accord in the temple, and breaking bread from house to house..."* (Acts 2:46).

1. *Continually renewed.* The house church keeps coming back no matter how many methods are tried and no matter what new expressions of Christianity seem to come to the forefront. During the 1900s, Christianity seemed to build bigger and better buildings to preach, worship, teach, fellowship, and serve. We added more seats, better acoustics, brighter visual aids, and increasingly impressive, beautiful, and instructive symbols. It seemed modern technology couldn't wait to come up with innovative and astonishing breakthroughs in every new device. Yet when the Communists swept away all the church's buildings and advances, the house church survived the rape of modernism and the ravages of the evil one—and not only did it survive, but it thrived and became the victorious tool of Jesus Christ, who promised, *"...the gates of hell shall not prevail against it"* (Matt. 16:18 KJV).

2. *Culturally relevant.* A lot of things the church does in ministry will not work in all cultures, in all circumstances, and among all people. Sunday school bus ministry wouldn't work among tribes in the upper Amazon, nor in any culture that doesn't have mass transportation. D.L. Moody used a horse-drawn wagon in the streets of Chicago over 150 years ago, but it was appropriate for the culture of his day.

The video venue churches can't work in some societies because they are not technologically advanced enough. Just today I heard millennials laugh at going to a church where they watched a pastor preach on a screen. An evangelistic method is the adaptation of eternal principles to preach the Gospel to people in their culture, meeting their needs in a specific place at a particular time. So, what doesn't work everywhere? It is almost all the non-inspired evangelistic tools or methods that the church has created.

The house church is never out of style because a house was not conceived to be stylish. Also, the house church is never out of date because from the beginning people have needed a house to live in. The house church is never out of place because the very first family needed a house to raise their children. So, a house will be needed by the family of God as long as a house has been needed by a physical family.

3. *First experience.* Almost everyone understands family and houses. Most of us began our life in a family and we grew up with a roof over our head. Most are born into a family, so we can understand a family church. Most grow up in a home, so we can understand a home church. Most have lived in a house, so we can understand what it means to live in a house with others. Therefore, we naturally understand a house church.

CAN CHURCH PLANTS COME FROM CHURCH SPLITS?

The Bible does not give illustrations or principles concerning a church split. As a matter of fact, the Bible does not even prohibit the church from splitting or separating.

There are pictures of a church split drawn from nature. When God created plants, bushes, and trees, God said, *"Let the land sprout with vegetation—every sort of seed-bearing plant, and trees that grow seed-bearing fruit. These seeds will then produce the kinds of plants and trees from which they came"* (Gen. 1:11 NLT). God suggested a natural split would come when a life-bearing cell would split, causing two cells.

God made the same prediction concerning all animals, birds, and fish (see Gen. 1:26). The same process took place in human beings (see Gen. 1:27). The division of cells was natural and planned by God. But some churches have split, and that division was apparently not planned or directed by God. However, could church splits be classi-fied within the providence of God because *"...all things work together for good..."* (Rom. 8:28)?

There was an east–west schism in A.D. 1054 when the Roman Catholic Church centered in Rome split from the Eastern Orthodox Church centered in Istanbul, Turkey. Two major Christian branches developed and grew apart. That split was caused by doctrinal, practi-cal, and personality differences.

Another great split happened when Martin Luther tacked the 95 theses on the door of All Saints' Church in Wittenberg, Germany, on October 31, 1517. Out of that split from the Roman Catholic Church came the Lutheran Church, followed by other groups in Protestant Christianity that protested the Roman Catholic views on communion and/or the forgiveness of sins. The writings of Luther were significant in paving the way for the rise of the new Protestant church movement.

The Baptists split from the Congregational churches in Massa-chusetts in 1638 when Roger Williams was expelled from the colony because he was spreading "dangerous ideas." Fearing arrest, Williams fled and began the colony in Rhode Island at Providence Planta-tion in 1636. Two years later, he founded the First Baptist Church of Providence in America.

The Northern and Southern Baptist Convention split in 1845 at the First Baptist Church in Augusta, Georgia. The northern church, that is, the American Baptist Missionary Union, refused to ordain or license a man who was a slaveholder in 1844. The issue was slavery. The following year, in 1845, southern churches created the Southern Baptist Convention to "preserve the southern culture."

The issue of slavery was not politically solved until the Civil War and the Emancipation Proclamation of 1863. Even after the Civil War, the repercussions of slavery were felt in the United States.

In 1954, at the Southern Baptist Convention in St. Louis, Missouri, "identification reconciliation" was practiced. Two symbolical vice presidents of the Southern Baptist Convention stood on the platform. The white vice president washed the feet of the black vice president and said, "My grandfathers were slave owners, our fathers practiced racial discrimination, and my generation has continued segregation. That was sin." Then the white Southern Baptist vice president asked the black vice president to forgive his great grandfather, his grandfather, and the present generation for their racial views of segregation. He was following the biblical example of Nehemiah, who faced the challenge of building the walls in Jerusalem by confessing his sins and the sins of his forefathers that caused the captivity of Jerusalem (see Neh. 1:6-11). Daniel prayed the same prayer of identification and repentance (see Dan. 9:3-19).

There was a separation between the Calvary Chapel movement founder, Chuck Smith, in the late 1960s from the Vineyard movement, founded by Kenn Gulliksen and John Wimber. The split was primarily between Smith and Wimber. Smith, who had been ordained in the Four Square denomination, was moving away from extreme Pentecostal expressions of signs and wonders and the traditional Pentecostal expressions of Christianity. Wimber was moving in the opposite direction. In 1982, they agreed to bless one another and go their separate ways. Smith led Calvary Chapel, and Gulliksen and Wimber led the Vineyard churches.

There was a split between Paul and Barnabas after their first successful missionary journey. The split was so deep that they decided not to work together on the second tour.

After some time Paul said to Barnabas, "Let's go back and visit each city where we previously preached the word of the Lord, to see how the new believers are doing." Barnabas agreed and wanted to take along John Mark. But Paul disagreed strongly, since John Mark had deserted them in Pamphylia and had not continued with them in their work. Their disagreement was so sharp that they separated. Barnabas took John Mark with him and sailed for Cyprus. Paul chose Silas, and as he left, the believers entrusted him to the Lord's gracious care. Then he traveled throughout Syria and Cilicia, strengthening the churches there (Acts 15:36-41 NLT).

Note the following: Barnabas started out as the leader in the first missionary tour. His name was listed first: *"...Barnabas and Saul..."* (Acts 13:7). Later Paul became the leader: *"Paul and Barnabas..."* (Acts 13:46 NLT). Was there a struggle for leadership that caused this split? Also, was there a question of nepotism? John Mark was related to Barnabas; they were cousins (see Col. 4:10).

Perhaps it was John Mark's youthfulness that Paul distrusted. Because John Mark left them in the middle of the first missionary journey, Paul was not willing to trust him again.

Whatever the reason, the split led to the multiplication of churches and ministry. Barnabas went back to Cyprus, his home area, to strengthen the churches. Paul went back to Turkey, his home area, and began other new churches.

ATTITUDES ABOUT CHURCH SPLITS

Remember, one of the characteristics of churches is they change as they grow. A young sprout changes into a bush and then it may develop limbs, a trunk, and finally fruit. Similarly, as a church grows older, especially moving into a second generation, changes occur in its governance and relationships. Sometimes a church will divide naturally; other times it can be contentious, and even there have been angry splits.

As obnoxious as a church split may appear, there have been times when God was leading a group of people to leave the mother church and plant a new one.

However, the attitude behind a church split goes against the traditional attitude in Christianity, "a church should never split." Because Jesus said, "...*I will build My church*...," most think it is presumptuous to even think about splitting a church (Matt. 16:18). If Jesus formed the church, how could man split it? A church split flies in the face of Jesus' prayer, "...*so they may be one as we are one*" (John 17:22 NLT).

As we go through this chapter, it will be difficult to analyze church splits because they usually are not born of reason and logic, but of emotions and deep feelings.

Any pastor of a group of people that leads to a split, even over the smallest issue, will have their motives doubted by the general public as well as the church community.

The problem with church splits is that sometimes when a group leaves, those who stay try to "vote out" those who left because of wrong attitudes.

I once interviewed a pastor and asked, "How many churches have you started?"

He responded, "Several...but not by design." He smiled to let me know that two or three groups had left his church because they disagreed with what he was doing and/or believed.

This brings up the following question: Is there a proper way to split a congregation so that glory is brought to God? Some say "no"; others say that it is inevitable when the existing church changes its doctrine, lifestyle, and/or purpose.

WHY CHURCH SPLITS ARE INEVITABLE

The church is symbolically portrayed as a body in Scripture. That wonderful illustration shows how the church works together in coordination and interaction so that all organs depend on each other for happiness and the pursuit of life's necessities. David writes of the body: *"You made all the delicate inner parts of my body...making me so wonderfully complex..."* (Ps. 139:13-14 NLT). This suggests that God planned the cell's DNA and all the muscles, organs, and nerves to interact with one another and arranged for the interaction between the physical, the emotional, and the mental. The body is a wonderful picture of how a church should minister.

But there is also a negative picture that is seldom mentioned. Because of the fall of humanity into sin, God cursed the earth and everything in it. Now the human body is susceptible to disease, weariness, decay, and death. The physical body is also corrupt and has evil or destructive impulses because of the fall of mankind (see Gen. 3). The human body can be debilitated by the smallest disease that plants itself in the smallest cell. That disease can lead to pain, physical weakness, and dysfunction. Disease and also accidents can debilitate and cause premature death. The body can lose its hearing, sight, and balance, as well as its ability to walk, feed itself, and talk.

Diseases can unknowingly seep their way into a church body, creating disunity and dysfunction and even possibly leading to the death of the church. Diseases can cause a church to lose its vision of ministry, its ability to hear the directing voice of God, or its ability to take the Gospel to the unsaved. The church body can choose or gravitate toward the wrong goals, wrong expressions of worship, and even wrong doctrinal assumptions. Because disease can be so subtle, the church body can lose its ability to know itself, to operate, or even to maintain its community. And when disease runs its course, a church body can die. Is there a time to bury a local church because it has died? If a church body is in hospice, should active members try to revive it or bury it?[1]

What about an accident? The human body will inevitably have broken bones, cuts, crushed organs, and/or concussions. Church bodies should be prepared for inevitable tragedies. If a church body is so wounded that it can never regain its strength or viability, should active members remain? Should they try to revive a nonfunctioning body, or should they become involved in a new challenge with promise, vitality, and vision of doing something great for God?

Is there a natural growth cycle in a church body that reflects the growth cycle in human bodies? Do church bodies have limitations like children's bodies but at the same time manifest unparalleled energy? Can a church body have poor coordination, small muscles, and limbs that have not been disciplined or trained?

Can a church body be like a teenage body that is almost mature but struggles with desires and vision? Can a church body be similar to a senior citizen's frail body?

Have some church bodies gotten so old that they are past the age of reproduction? Are some old church bodies saddled with weak muscles that cannot run, and when they do, they get tired? Do old church bodies need more rest to renew their energy? There are some good traits in mature church bodies that are smart, efficient, productive, and that reproduce themselves in another church.

We need to ask the question asked of Ezekiel: *"Son of man, can these bones become living people again?"* (Ezek. 37:3 NLT). The answer is "yes!" God can do anything. Dead bones can live again with flesh and muscle. They can come together again miraculously.

Yes, dead churches can be revived by a man of God who breathes the life of evangelism and passion back into a dead church. But church bodies usually do not revive themselves. They do not see the error of their ways, nor do they see where they were derailed from the straight and narrow path of carrying out the Great Commission. There must be an outside force that turns them around. There must be a new voice calling them to repentance and to turn around. Someone must breathe new life (the life of God) into dead bodies so they can live again.

Old people don't get out of a hospice bed to begin over again. That is not God's pattern for His creation and for humanity. But does God do it for old church bodies? Probably not! God starts the cycle over again and again and again. God begins with the sperm of a man joining to the egg of a woman to create a new life, with a new body and a new future. Just as God recreates a new physical body for humans, so God recreates a new spiritual church body.

Jesus becomes incarnate in each new church; He is resurrected to new spiritual life. He lives again to carry out the Great Commission.

ADVANTAGES OF PLANTING CHURCHES FROM SPLITS

When one group leaves or splits from the original church, they usually bring financial commitment to the new church. Finances are more than money; they usually indicate a dedication of purpose, time, and resources. Therefore, finances show evidence of life.

The new church has a core of people. Usually, those who join together to leave also have the commitment to join together to serve in the new church.

Jerry Falwell Sr. was converted at the Park Avenue Baptist Church in Lynchburg, Virginia, in January 1952. The pastor who was responsible for his salvation, Paul Donaldson, committed sexual immorality and left the church. That sin was handled in a proper way. However, the authorities at Baptist Bible College in Springfield, Missouri, had assigned a new pastor for the church and sent him to Lynchburg. A core of faithful believers at Park Avenue Baptist Church was disappointed in the replacement and found evangelistic fervor was not as evident as in Paul Donaldson. The replacement pastor didn't separate himself from the world as the previous pastor had, and there was little passion to continue the worldwide missionary endeavor.

The core of 50 believers called for a vote concerning the new pastoral leadership. They wanted the church to call a pastor, not accept the pastor assigned by the authorities in Springfield. There was a continuous congregational meeting at which county deputy sheriffs were present to maintain order during the meeting. When the core calling for the change had lost the vote that evening, those remaining at Park Avenue Baptist Church immediately voted to "kick out" the 50 members who had caused the uproar.

The core of 50 people contacted Jerry Falwell and organized Thomas Road Baptist Church on June 21, 1956. The rest is history.

New churches growing out of splits usually have a core of committed mature Christians who will give stability and vision to the new church.

Another advantage in the new church plant is they usually have a closely knit group of people who will pray together, sacrifice together, and rally around the common cause of carrying out the Great Commission.

DISADVANTAGES OF CHURCH SPLITS

Many times when two churches split, it leaves a poor reputation in the community and among other Christians. This is quite an obstacle for both churches to overcome and sometimes a barrier to future ministry.

Another disadvantage is the bitterness between the two separating groups. That "root of bitterness" may sour both churches and hinder them from fulfilling God's purpose for their life.

Sometimes the new church will not be planted for evangelism or to carry out the Great Commission; sometimes it is planted for negative reasons. Perhaps they are retaliating against the former group or are separating to foster a "pet" doctrine or for a narrow church purpose. A split can come from any reason other than the true nature and purpose of a church.

Sometimes the people who could not get along with those in the previous church have an attitude problem. The contentious nature in the old church may carry over into the new church plant, and the new congregation has the same embryonic problem as the old one.

Sometimes continued opposition by the old or original group of people will hinder the new church and keep it from growing and fulfilling its purpose.

RESISTING A CHURCH SPLIT

What should be done when there is a possibility of a church split? Because of the unity of Christianity and because the common core of a church is Jesus Christ, every group should take every measure possible to keep the light of the church candlestick shining brightly. Remember, Jesus is the light of the world. He indwells every believer, plus He indwells the local assembly.

Therefore, it is the responsibility of every church member to pray for unity, preserve unity, give their whole allegiance to correct biblical doctrine, and practice pure living. In addition to that, they should be committed to carrying out the church's doctrine and purpose. When there is an offense, those who are mature should go to the offended in the spirit of meekness to carry out New Testament reconciliation (see Matt. 5:22-25; 18:15-18; Rom. 13:18-21).

However, when God's blessing is removed from a church, which means His anointing for ministry and outreach is gone, it is time for zealous believers to do something about it. If they believe their church no longer qualifies as a New Testament church, or if they believe their church is no longer carrying out the mandate of a church, it is their obligation to become a part of a group that will go elsewhere to fulfill that obligation.

After all is said and done, the final step of church controversy is usually a church split. When a local church's existence is threatened by impurity or disobedience to the Word of God, perhaps there is no other route but beginning another church.

WHEN SHOULD A SPLIT OCCUR?

A church split is justified when the purpose of the church is compromised. When does this happen? Some maintain that Christians ought to remain in an existing church with problems because they can still win souls and influence some people. However, recognize that a layman can only do so much to influence a church. He is only one voice among many. If his voice is drowned out and not heeded, perhaps he should go where his light will be most effective.

Remember, the pastor and board leadership will have the most influence on a church's direction in doctrine, ministry, and purity. Laymen contribute by adding a voice, counseling with leadership, and voting leadership into place. But when an individual or group no longer has influence, what should they do?

People usually remain in a dead church because of their friends, the facilities, or the resources and equipment that is available to them. However, when believers lose their freedom of ministry and Christian expression in their church, maybe it is time to go help plant a new church.

A church split is justified when church doctrine is compromised. A New Testament church is bound together by its harmony and agreement in doctrine. Even at the Jerusalem Council when they disagreed over doctrine, the churches were strong enough to override the diverse nature of opinions and rally around the Great Commission. However, when the church is growing in knowledge and evangelism, there should be no disagreement about doctrine. Yet, Christians have different personalities; their thought patterns differ, and feelings are expressed differently for different reasons. No matter where a believer finds himself, he will never completely agree with all the other believers in a church. But are they justified in splitting a church just because of a disagreement over a minor issue of doctoral practice? Remember, pure doctrine is not the ultimate or only purpose of a church. However, when the cohesive group of people are held together only by pure doctrine, they tend to argue over major or minor variations of dead orthodoxy. This in turn may lead them to unjustified church splits because of disagreement over doctrine.

Therefore, new churches should be planted and people should leave the present church only when it can be demonstrated that the former alliance has broken fidelity with New Testament doctrine and/or purity of living.

Purity of Christian living is another factor that can lead to a church split. Remember, God will not hold any Christian blameless who sins because He demands purity in each member as well as in the church itself. When a church allows obvious sin to continue with no attempt to correct it, God will remove His candlestick for light of blessing from that church. Therefore, a new church is justified only when sin in the existing church keeps it from fulfilling its basic purpose of carrying out the Great Commission.

The following cautions are in order. Remember, every church has some evil present in its members and in the group. No individual or group of people is completely pure in doctrine, lifestyle, and attitude.

We should confess that we are sinners and need the forgiveness of God.

When a church is attempting to deal with a sin issue or doctrinal issue, no split should be considered and individuals should not plan to leave the church.

Also, remember there is probably more sin in the fringe members of the church than in those who are active in its life or leadership. Therefore, a split is justified when a church allows public sin to remain in its leadership or when it accepts wrong doctrine. When public sin destroys a church, a new church must be established.

ATTITUDES DURING A CHURCH SPLIT

A denominational official once said to me, "You conservatives are always splitting churches." He was criticizing evangelicals because they put more emphasis on biblical doctrine and standards than people in traditional churches. But there is a reason why conservative churches will split from a dying denominational church. Very few liberals ever split a church because they focus on relationships and give attention to fellowship. That is their priority. However, evangelicals believe a church's foundation is doctrinal and that purity of life is necessary for the blessing of God. Therefore, when doctrine or purity is ignored, evangelicals will emphasize the essentials, realizing relationships and fellowship depend on doctrinal commitment to the Word of God and purity of life.

1.   Keep issues centered on doctrine, not personalities. Too many church splits center on the people who become the issue. Yes, people are concerned about doctrine and people fight over doctrine, but they make themselves the focus of the issue, rather than doctrine. Too often, personal feelings obscure doctrinal truth.

2. The motivation to start a new church should be to fulfill the Great Commission. Even though you want doctorial purity, is doctrinal purity a basis to start a new church? Probably not! Also, harmony is not the ultimate purpose to begin a new congregation. A new church, even when founded on doctrinal truth, will flounder if it is not focused on evangelism.

3. A church split should follow scriptural patterns of dealing with grievances. When one Christian has a charge against another, they should face the other person with the issue. Forget feelings, passion, and personalities. Focus on the issue.

Take someone with you when airing grievances to another person. The Bible directs, *"By the mouth of two or three witnesses every word shall be established"* (2 Cor. 13:1).

Next, take the issue to the church, that is, before a committee of deacons or pastoral staff that represents the church. Sometimes the issue will even have to be taken before the entire church body.

Always follow the constitution and bylaws of the church when dealing with grievances. Make sure that the issues are clear, objective, and understood by all parties. It is best to write them down and agree upon what has been written.

No church split should be attempted if the issue has not been dealt with by the church as a whole. Discuss it rationally and calmly. Pray together for the mind of God and the future direction of the church. But even before you pray about it, examine the Scriptures and then determine what God is saying about the issue at hand.

4. Keep all motives pure. It is easy for jealously, strife, and hard feelings to influence a decision. Keep a sweet spirit. Remember when you disagree with another believer that you are both born again by the same blood of Jesus Christ. You both have Christ in your hearts, and there should be unity in God's house.

But if the opposing group is apostate, meaning they have denied the Word of God, you are not dealing with fellow believers; you are dealing with lost people. Therefore, you cannot treat them as believers, but you have an obligation to live honestly before them as a Christian.

Do not win the battle to lose the war. Some church splits have been so hateful that both sides destroy their reputation in the community. After the severance, neither side is able to win lost people to Christ because both of them have displayed non-Christian behavior.

Judge every action by the long look. Ask yourself what the new church will look like because of the split and what the remaining church will look like. A new church will have to live in the community for a long time after the split.

When a church battles for its existence, many times it gets a reputation of being comprised of "fighters." The problem with that type of reputation is that people will see the confrontation before seeing Jesus Christ.

The church should always be known for the truth, not for being militant against other believers. At the same time, both sides must be loving and should pray for one another.

CONCLUSION

I do not encourage church splits. However, I do recognize that there are times when these things happen. There are situations that cannot be redefined, and there are issues in churches that cannot be solved. Therefore, there will be church splits. So, my prayer is, "...*that they may be one...*" (John 17:11).

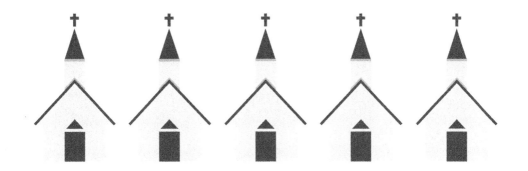

TOOLS FOR SUCCESSFUL CHURCH PLANTING

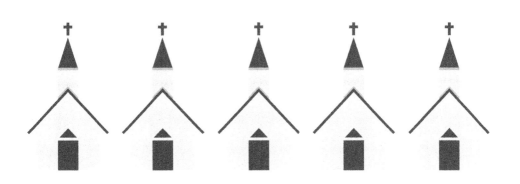

THE NATURE OF THE CHURCH DETERMINES HOW IT IS PLANTED

Jesus used a normal, everyday word—*ecclesia*—to introduce the idea of church to His disciples. *Ecclesia* means "assembly" or "gathering." In its day, it meant a political, business, or family gathering.

Jesus planned to gather His followers together with a twofold action. First, He would invite them to leave or "repent" and no longer live in the world, for the world, or by the principles of the world. Instead, they would gather into His assembly. The second action was that Jesus would gather His people to be with Him, serve Him, and worship God.

Jesus introduced the idea, "*...I will build My church...*" (Matt. 16:18). He could have used the word *grow*, saying instead, "I will grow My church." That would have implied growth by internal forces from the seeds planted.

Jesus could have said, "I will supervise My church." That would have suggested His outward energy would do it all.

Jesus could have said, "I will expand My church." That would have suggested a business model and focused only on what the church had to offer.

Also, Jesus didn't say, "I will organize My church." That would have emphasized outward things like programs, services, and committees.

But Jesus said, *"...I will build My church..."* (Matt. 16:18). The word *build* is in the active voice: Jesus will continually build His church. That involved all of the above actions. Jesus will plant the church and let it grow according to the energy of the seed of the Gospel. Some will be worshiping churches, others will be Bible study churches, and others will be evangelistic churches. Some will be churches of small groups, churches of ministry, or churches of healing and restoration.

Jesus meant that He would be its source of life, energy, and direction. All spiritual energy would come from Him. When Jesus used the phrase, *"build My church,"* He was describing both outward energy from Him and inward energy from the members in that church. The church would grow both as an organism and an organizationn. It would grow like His human body but also like a man-made organization.

But notice the possessive pronoun *my*. The church will belong to Jesus. He will be its inner life and vitality. He will be its organization and management. He will be the force that gets the church going in the morning, ministering throughout the day, and resting as night approaches.

The church will be Jesus.

The following definition of the church will be used in this book and is proposed here to guide the planting of local churches:

A church is an assembly of professing followers of Jesus Christ; He lives in them, and they minister under the discipline of the Word of God. A church is organized to carry out the Great Commission by evangelism, teaching, fellowship, worship, administering the ordinances, and reflecting the spiritual gift of ministry.

This work will use two ways to present the church. First, by *definition*, which draws the parameters of a church, sharpens the purpose of the church, and focuses on the nature and ministry of the church. Second, a church will be *described* in eight pictures as presented in Scriptures.

A *definition* will sharpen and clarify the purpose of the church. A *description* will broaden our understanding of the church by applying its nature and ministry.

DEFINITION: THE NECESSITY OF LEARNING CHURCH

The church planter should understand that only Jesus Christ can successfully plant and establish a New Testament church. When He said, *"...I will build My church...,"* you must realize that the church begins with Christ and is indwelt by Christ (Matt. 16:18). He indwells every believer and is the source of what must be taught. You will learn that new believers are baptized by water immersion into a church because they have been spiritually baptized into Jesus Christ, dying with Him, being buried with Him in death, and being raised again to new life.

Many church plants fail because they lack new life from Jesus Christ. Church planters may understand organization and may receive the authority of a denomination or sponsoring church, but unless they are rightly related to Jesus Christ, they cannot plant a successful church, nor can they cause it to grow. Remember, Jesus is the church, *"which is His body"* (Eph. 1:23).

However, when the doctrine of the church reflects the Scriptures and the founding pastor or team are rightly related to Jesus Christ, then they can successfully plant a New Testament church.

Some feel the primary aim of a church is Bible teaching—they even call themselves a Bible church. Yes, every member of the church must be taught the *"things that I have commanded you"* (Matt. 28:20). Church members must be disciples, and a disciple is a follower of Jesus.

Some feel the primary purpose of a church is to nurture and care for new believers. While that is one of the aims, that is only a means to an end. The aim of a church is to carry out the Great Commission—to preach the Gospel to all people, everywhere, at all times.

Some feel the primary purpose of a church is worship. The Presbyterians in their children's catechism says, "The chief end of man is to glorify God (1) and enjoy Him forever."[1] Yes, the act of worship must go on in a New Testament church, but the act of planting a church is worship to God. In one sense, everything we do is worship to God, and that is reflected in a local church. But church planting is much more than worship.

There are others who feel that the purpose of a church is body life, relationship, or fellowship. They see examples in the early church fellowshipping from house to house, and they see biblical references to fellowshipping with one another. Yes, fellowship is an outgrowth of a church, but it is not the main purpose of the church.

Also, a physical structure or building is not a church. Whether a local church gathers in a home, a grass hut, or a magnificent cathedral does not matter. The structure is not the church. God may come and manifest Himself in that structure, but foundation, bricks, and lumber are only a means to an end.

Again, remember the church is Jesus Christ; it is His body here on earth. When people hear about a local church, they should think of Jesus Christ. When they enter a local church, they should experience His presence. And when a church evangelizes or ministers in any way, it should be the hands and feet of Jesus who are ministering to other people.

1. *A church is an assembly of baptized believers.* The church began on the Day of Pentecost when Peter preached and *"they that gladly received his word were baptized: and the same day there were added unto them about three thousand souls"* (Acts 2:41). That phrase "added unto them" suggests there were 120 in the Upper Room praying for Pentecost. But after the great sermon by Peter, they numbered 3,120.

Don't forget baptism. How did they get into the church? Through the first symbol of membership: they were baptized.

Baptism is more than a religious mantra. Believer's baptism is identification with Jesus Christ Himself. Paul reminds us of the spiritual nature of baptism: *"For we died and were buried with Christ by baptism. And just as Christ was raised from the dead by the glorious power of the Father, now we also may live new lives. Since we have been united with Him in His death, we will also be raised to life as He was"* (Rom. 6:4-5 NLT).

As a baby, I was sprinkled in a Presbyterian church in Savannah, Georgia. I don't know the date or the place and was never told about it. When I became a student pastor of Westminster Presbyterian Church in Savannah in 1952, I led people to Christ and baptized them by sprinkling. That was my heritage and what I was taught to do.

In 1954, I attended Dallas Theological Seminary and the first Sunday there went to First Baptist Church. I was drawn by the warm evangelistic preaching and the inviting nature of the church.

After attending for a few months, Dr. W.A. Criswell preached on Romans 6:4-5 and said, "There is no water in this verse." I knew that Romans 6 referred to spiritual baptism, meaning when Jesus died, I died with Him. When Jesus was raised from the dead on the third day, I was raised with Him and received new life in Jesus. That is the saving death of Christ and is called the "vicarious substitutionary atonement."

Dr. Criswell ended his sermon that evening by saying, "If when Jesus died, you died..." He repeated it dramatically three times. With a sudden climatic exclamation, he said, "If you died with Jesus in His death, why don't you tell the world in water?"

For the next few minutes, he preached the necessity of immersion from its spiritual picture. For the first time, I saw that when Jesus died, I died with Him; when He was raised, I received new life in Him. Eventually, I submitted myself to believer's baptism by immersion.

Every New Testament church will have some in their midst who are not saved, even though they were baptized by immersion. There was Simon the sorcerer in the church at Samaria (see Acts 8:18-24). Apparently, he was not saved until confronted by Peter, who said, "...your heart is not right in the sight of God" (Acts 8:21). So Simon responded, "Pray to the Lord for me..." (Acts 8:24). If the early church can have an unsaved person who deceives everyone, so can every church after that.

Paul knew that in the church in Corinth, someone was not saved, which is why he said, "Examine yourselves to see if your faith is genuine..." (2 Cor. 13:5 NLT).

Because Christ died for all, especially every member in your community, every new believer should follow the spiritual example and be baptized like Jesus and submit to the spiritual nature of baptism by identifying in His death, burial, and resurrection. Remember, there is no record of a baptized believer in the New Testament who was not associated with a local church. Therefore, it is doubtful that any Christian should live his/her Christian life for himself/herself and by himself/herself without being a member of a New Testament church.

> ## WHAT KEEPS A GROUP OF PEOPLE FROM BECOMING A NEW TESTAMENT CHURCH?
>
> 1 Wrong doctrine
> 2 Unbiblical leadership
> 3 An abundance of unsaved members
> 4. Organized for the wrong purpose
> 5. Tolerance of obvious sins/sinners in the church

2. *A church has the unique presence of Jesus Christ.* Remember, the church is more than an organization; it is an organism. The church is the life of Jesus Christ. He reminded us while on earth, *"For where two or three are gathered together in My name, I am there in the midst of them"* (Matt. 18:20). When He sent people out to carry out the Great Commission, He said, *"...I am with you always, even to the end of the age..."* (Matt. 28:20).

When Christ rebuked the seven churches in the Book of Revelation, He had something to say against each of them. He rebuked the church at Ephesus because *"they had lost their first love"* (see Rev. 2:4). He challenged them, *"...Turn back to Me and do the works you did at first. If you don't repent, I will come and remove your lampstand from its place among the churches"* (Rev. 2:5 NLT). The lampstand, or candlestick holder, is the light in that church, and of course the light is Jesus Christ. His testimony is light around the world. How was the church threatened? Jesus said that if they didn't love Him with all their heart, He would not live among them.

In the Old Testament, the word *Ichabod* was used to describe when the Spirit of God left the temple. In Ezekiel chapters 7 through

irit of God is lifted up over the Ark of the Covenant, then
ne door" leading into the temple. Next, the Spirit of God
...ed up over the gate to the city of Jerusalem and finally above to
the Mount of Olives that overlooks Jerusalem. And from that place
the Spirit of God left and returned to Heaven.

Just as the presence of God left the physical temple in the Old
Testament, so the presence of God can leave a local church today
when they deny God's purpose for the church and reject the things
God has for them.

EVIDENCE THAT A CHURCH IS INDWELT BY JESUS CHRIST

1. Souls are being saved.
2. The Word of God is being preached with power.
3. A genuine spirit of love exists.
4. Fellowship that builds up Christians is present.
5. A mature believer can sense the presence of God when the church comes together.

3. *The church must be under the authority of the Word of God.* No
church is the final authority, nor is it the determination of truth.
Every church must put itself under the teachings of the Scriptures
with a purpose to know them, live by them, and fulfill them in its
preaching and ministry. Notice that the early church "...*continued steadfastly in the apostles' doctrine...*" (Acts 2:42). By placing itself
under the Word of God, a church places itself under the authority of
God Himself.

When the pastor/teacher applies the Bible to his/her life, he or she
attempts not only to live by its direction, but to fulfill the commands
and manifest the power that comes through the indwelling Word.

4. *A church must be organized to carry out the Great Commission.*
The purpose of a church is not just to worship, teach Scriptures,

fellowship, minister to one another, or even minister humanitarian needs to the world. The purpose of a church is to carry out the last commands of Jesus Christ (see Chapter 4). The early church did this. *"And daily in the temple, and in every house, they did not cease teaching and preaching Jesus as the Christ"* (Acts 5:42). They did this first in the homes and second in the temple. That meant they did it in small groups or *cells*, which might be Sunday school classes or home Bible studies. But they also did it corporately in large groups in a format called "celebration." This is worshiping the Lord together each Lord's Day.

Because the early church organized itself to carry out the Great Commission, notice what their enemies said: *"...you have filled Jeru-salem with your doctrine..."* (Acts 5:28). The enemies were saying the church had become the talk of the town. Unsaved people were talking about the activities of the church and so were businesses, political figures, and other organizations. They were discussing how individuals in the church were being transformed.

One of the reasons local churches fail is because they do not organize themselves to carry out the Great Commission. There are many good things such as worship, teaching the Bible, fellowshipping, and serving humanity. The church will eventually fail if it does not focus on winning men and women, boys and girls, to Jesus Christ.

5. *A church must exercise the ordinances.* There were two ordinances given to the local church: baptism and the Lord's Table. Today, many interdenominational groups and even individuals are baptizing or partaking in the Lord's Table out of need or desire. The New Testament seems to picture baptism and the Lord's Table as being administered only among believers through local churches. In First Corinthians 11, Paul says four times, *"When you come together...,"* suggesting believers were assembled for the Lord's Table (see 1 Cor. 11:18,20,33).

Baptism is the door into the local church. Just as a new believer is spiritually baptized into the Body of Jesus Christ and His salvation, so new believers should be water-baptized into membership of a local body of Jesus Christ after they are saved.

The Lord's Table is symbolic of continual fellowship with Jesus Christ. When believers break bread together, it is symbolic of eating the Bread of Life. Remember Jesus said, *"I am the bread of life. Whoever comes to Me will never be hungry again..."* (John 6:35 NLT). This is a reference to initial salvation, but a person should partake of the Lord's Table on a regular basis, for that is reflective of continuing growth and fellowship with Christ.

The cup was symbolic of the spilt blood of Jesus Christ. When the Lord said, *"Drink ye all of it,"* the emphasis was not on all the liquid in the cup but all believers drinking together (Matt. 26:27 KJV). They "came together," reflecting the church, which is life *together.*

6. *A church reflects spiritual gifts.* Paul teaches that in every body there are many members—some for honor, and others with less honor (see 1 Cor. 12:22-25). Some members of the physical body are more necessary than others, such as the eye, the tongue, and the hand. In the spiritual body of the church, God suggests spiritual abilities by different believers carry out different functions in the local church body. *"Now these are the gifts Christ gave to the church: the apostles, the prophets, the evangelists, and the pastors and teachers"* (Eph. 4:11 NLT).

But there were many other spiritual gifts beyond those listed in the above verse. *"A spiritual gift is given to each of us so we can help each other"* (1 Cor. 12:7 NLT). Remember, *"our bodies have many parts, and God has put each part just where He wants it"* (1 Cor. 12:18 NLT). And why is that? *"...So that all the members care for each other"* (1 Cor. 12:25).

God raises up leaders to direct His church to accomplish His purpose. Those leaders are called "apostles," "prophets," "evangelists," "pastors," and "teachers." Those different offices have gifts to carry out their tasks. These gifts were given to them by God. For a complete study of spiritual gifts, see First Corinthians 12, Romans 12, and Ephesians 4.

God will raise up leaders to give focus and direction when the church begins to form. That's an indication that God wants the church to organize and move forward to carry out the Great Commission.

THE NATURE OF A CHURCH DETERMINES HOW IT IS PLANTED			
PICTURE		**CENTRAL TRUTH**	
1.	Body	1.	Unity
2.	Building	2.	Indwelling
3.	Bride	3.	Intimacy
4.	Flock	4.	Provision
5.	Garden (vine)	5.	Union
6.	Family	6.	Identity
7.	Priesthood	7.	Service

In the first section of this chapter, we saw the *definition* of the church, which analyzes the focus of a church and limits or eliminates other entities from that definition. Remember, definitions are found in dictionaries and/or encyclopedias, and they give information about the entity by telling you what is and what is not being defined.

By definition, a local church is not a high school Bible club. While members of the club may love one another, nurture one another, and teach one another, they do not carry out the functions of a New Testament church. The students do not identify with it through baptism, nor are they organized to carry out the purpose of a church.

The Gideons International have an outstanding ministry of placing Bibles in hotels, motels, and among students and military members. A local Gideon camp is not a local church, although they function to win people to Christ, spread God's Word abroad, and carry out general Christian purposes. An individual member of the Gideons may grow from working with the Gideons. However, a Gideon camp is not organized to carry out the Great Commission by baptizing according to the Great Commission.

Now let us look at a description of a church. Whereas a definition narrows our understanding of a church, a description broadens it. Rather than analyzing and restricting what a church is, a description will compare it to many entities that have characteristics similar to those of a church. It communicates by pictures or metaphors.

1. *The church is described as a body.* Paul tells us that gifts are given to leaders to build up the church, the Body of Christ (see Eph. 4:12). The picture has the church growing in every way more and more like Christ, who is the head of His body, the church (see Eph. 4:12).

What does a head do for the body? Robert Saucy, in his book *The Church in God's Program*, says, "There are six aspects or principles how Christ the head of the church relates to the body: 1. Unity, 2. Diversity, 3. Mutuality, 4. Sovereign leadership, 5. Source of life, 6. Sustenance of life."[2]

Every Christian should give Christ first place in everything, and every church must do the same thing. Why? Because *"...all things were created through Him and for Him"* (Col. 1:16); *"He existed before anything else..."* (Col. 1:17 NLT); and *"...He holds all creation together"* (Col. 1:17 NLT). As a result, Christ purposes to be first in all things (see Col. 1:18).

That means when a church body is healthy, all of its parts should function properly and carry out the will of its head. When disease and sickness strike the body, usually they attack the greatest weakness in the body and then incapacitate the whole body. And the same thing happens in the local church: when individuals sin or when someone in leadership violates God's commandments, the whole body is disabled (see 1 Cor. 12:26). God describes the church as a body to teach that we need one another and should care for one another, love another, and grow together with God.

There seems to be five views about how the church relates to the Body of Christ. First, the church is the actual Body of Christ, making each local assembly equal to Christ Himself. However, the body is a description, not the actual physical Bbody of Christ.

Second, the figurative view implies that local churches are only similar to Christ's body with no organic connection. Christ indwelling the believer is only a picture, so He indwells the local church as a picture.

Third, the Church is the Body of Christ in a spiritual sense. A church is spiritual when it has the life and power of Christ flowing in and through it.

Fourth, the church is His body in a localized sense. Each church represents the Body of Christ on this earth because Christ indwells each individual and manifests Himself in the corporate church. Therefore, the church is called "His localized presence on earth."

The fifth is the atmospheric presence of Christ. This is more than Christ dwelling in each individual believer; this is the indwelling presence of Jesus Christ in true believers and in the local church. When I travel to different churches, sometimes I feel a spirituality or power in certain local assemblies that I don't feel in others. That means in some churches they feel "dead," or there is "a weak" presence of Christ in that church. Why is that? Remember, revival is defined as "God pouring His presence on His people."[3] When individuals completely surrender to Jesus Christ to do His will and seek to obey Him in life and ministry, God anoints them and manifests His presence through them. That anointing carries into local churches.

2. *The church is described as the temple of God.* The church is described as a temple of God, as a growing edifice. Paul told the Ephesians, *"Together, we are His house, built on the foundation of the apostles and the prophets. And the cornerstone is Christ Jesus Himself. We are carefully joined together in Him, becoming a holy temple for the Lord. Through Him you Gentiles are also being made part of this dwelling where God lives by His Spirit"* (Eph. 2:20-22 NLT).

Remember that God said that each individual believer's body is the temple of the Holy Spirit (see 1 Cor. 3:16; 6:19). Therefore, every believer's body is a temple of the Holy Spirit when they come together corporately. And just as believers grow in grace and maturity, so the local church should grow in its ability to serve, becoming more mature and more effective in God's ministry.

In the Old Testament, Israel first had a tent called the "tabernacle" and second, a temple in which God was pleased to dwell among His people. The Bible describes Moses as doing exactly as God had commanded him in Exodus chapter 40. That involved setting up the walls of the tabernacle, putting furniture in its place, and placing the Ark of the Covenant in the Holy of Holies.

"Then the cloud covered the tabernacle, and the glory of the Lord filled the tabernacle" (Exod. 40:34 NLT). What a magnificent thing that God dwelt among His people. Today, God dwells in His church among His people. This describes the church as a temple.

Remember, a temple has three sections: first, the foundation; second, the cornerstone; and finally, the stone building blocks of which the building is made. According to Bob Saucy, "The apostles have laid the foundations by teaching the doctrines of Christ and bringing men into a relationship with him who is the only foundation that is laid. The church is not built upon a man or creed, but upon the person of the living Christ."[4]

The fact that the church is a temple exhorts us to live properly. Paul said, *"But let every man take heed how he buildeth thereupon…if any man build upon this foundation…every man's work shall be made manifest: for the day shall declare it, because it shall be revealed by fire; and the fire shall try every man's work of what sort it is"* (1 Cor. 3:10,12-13 KJV).

3. *The church is described as the bride of Christ.* John invites the readers of the Book of Revelation, *"Come, I will show you the bride, the Lamb's wife"* (Rev. 21:9). Paul expounds upon this truth when he says, *"For I am jealous for you with godly jealousy…"* (2 Cor. 11:2).

> *For the husband is head of the wife, as also Christ is head of the church; and He is the Savior of the body. Therefore, just as the church is subject to Christ, so let the wives be to their own husbands in everything. Husbands, love your wives, just as Christ also loved the church and gave Himself for her, that He might sanctify and cleanse her with the washing of water by the word, that He might present her to Himself a glorious church, not having spot or wrinkle or any such thing, but that she should be holy and without blemish. So husbands ought to love their own wives as their own bodies; he who loves his wife loves himself. For no one ever hated his own flesh, but nourishes and cherishes it, just as the Lord does the church. For we are members of His body, of His flesh and of His bones, "for this reason a man shall leave his father and mother and be joined to his wife, and the two shall become one flesh." This is a great mystery, but I speak concerning Christ and the church* (Ephesians 5:23-32).

The main truth about the Bride of Christ is our intimacy with and love for Jesus Christ. Why should we love Him with all our hearts? Because He first loved us completely and without measure.

We must learn about Jesus Christ so that we *"may be able to comprehend with all the saints, what is the width and length and depth and height—to know the love of Christ which passes knowledge"* (Eph. 3:18-19). When we understand how much Christ loved us, then we're able to respond to and love Him with all our hearts. Since He has given everything to us, we must give everything back to Him. And remember, the nature of love is giving: just as a bride gives herself to her husband, so we must give ourselves to Jesus Christ and serve Him through the church.

4.   *The church is described as the flock of God.* When Paul met with the elders in Ephesus, he challenged them, *"Therefore take heed to yourselves and to all the flock, among which the Holy Spirit has made you overseers, to shepherd the church of God which He purchased with His own blood"* (Acts 20:28).

The greatness of Psalm 23 shows Jesus' shepherd care over us. When we come into His church, He is the Shepherd who oversees the sheep in His fold.

Remember, the word *pastor* comes from *poimen*, which means "shepherd." So, the pastor of a local church is a shepherd of souls. Technically, they are the under-shepherd under Jesus Christ, who shepherds the flock.

There is a difference between the flock and the fold. Jesus noted this difference: *"I have other sheep, too, that are not in this sheep fold. I must bring them also. They will listen to My voice, and there will be one flock with one shepherd"* (John 10:16 NLT).

He seems to be using two different words to describe a gathering of believers. First was the *fold*, which describes the outward organization, and the second is *flock*, which describes the inner unity of the sheep in Jesus Christ. Overall, we can liken this picture to be the *organizational* church as opposed to the *organic* church.[5]

Since Christ is the Chief Shepherd, when He appears in the second coming, He will reward His faithful under-shepherds (see 1 Peter 5:4).

Donald McGavran says that the Great Commission is fulfilled by finding sheep (evangelism), folding sheep (baptizing), and feeding sheep (discipling or teaching). He goes on to say that "God wants countable lost persons found. The shepherd with 99 lost sheep who stays at home feeding or caring for them should not expect commendation. God will not be pleased by the excuse that His servant was doing something 'more spiritual than searching for stray sheep.' Nothing is more spiritual than the natural reconciliation of the lost to God."[6]

5. *The church is described as a garden.* A local church is reflective of a collection of several organic growing entities, for example, vines, plantings, farm, husbandry, and fruit trees.

A garden is a cultivated plot of ground where weeds and rocks are removed, seed is sown, and crops and fruit are harvested.

What does the description of the church as a garden tell us? Each Christian must depend on Christ alone as the only source of life, growth, and harvest. This is what Jesus meant when He said, *"Abide in Me, and I in you. As the branch cannot bear fruit of itself, unless it abides in the vine, neither can you, unless you abide in Me"* (John 15:4).

Did you see the double transference in that description? First of all, *"I in you"* implies that Christ is in the believer. That is His indwelling, or the source of power. The second transference is *"you in Me,"* which is our union with Jesus Christ in the heavenlies. We must be attached to Jesus Christ to get spiritual life and growth and to produce a harvest. This entails prayer, the study of the Word, meditation, and yieldedness to Jesus Christ. Both the vine (Christ) and the branches (Christians) make up the church, but spiritual power or fruit only flows one way. It comes from Christ through the believer.

Remember the purpose of the garden is fruit-bearing. And what is fruit? First, it is winning souls. Just as a fig tree produces figs and a grape vine produces grapes, so a Christian should lead another person to Jesus Christ.

But fruit-bearing is also related to character, hence the fruit of the Spirit (singular). Paul describes, *"But the Holy Spirit produces this kind of fruit in our lives: love, joy, peace, patience, kindness, goodness, faithfulness, gentleness, and self-control..."* (Gal. 5:22-23 NLT).

Don't forget that Jesus said the Father must prune the branches for the harvest to continue. *"I am the true grapevine, and My Father is the gardener. He cuts off every branch of Mine that doesn't produce fruit, and He prunes the branches that do bear fruit so they will produce even more"* (John 15:1-2 NLT).

Many things happen in a local church that hinder growth—things such as false doctrine, sin, unyieldedness, and self-will. But Jesus Christ prunes the branches (Christians) in His church to cut off and cut out things that strangle growth and limit fruit. The entire purpose is that the church will win souls, or that the vine will produce a harvest.

6. *The church is described as a family of God.* There are several pictures in the New Testament that describe Christians as children, sons, daughters, saints, sanctified ones, believers, disciples, brethren, sisters, and of course as family. All of these terms reflect relationship in a local church.

John describes how believers become God's children when they believe: *"But to all who believed Him and accepted Him, He gave the right to become children of God"* (John 1:12 NLT). What does he say about them? They are reborn (see John 1:13). In another place, Jesus describes being born into God's family: *"...You must be born again"* (John 3:7).

The church is a family, God is our Father in Heaven, and believers call one another brothers and sisters as members of the family of God.

7. *The church is described as a priesthood.* In the Old Testament, a Levite was set aside in the office of priesthood to serve God. When the church is described as a priesthood, it focuses attention on our serving God. Technically, Christ is the Priest for all believers. Paul reminds us, *"There is one God and one Mediator who can reconcile God and humanity—the man Christ Jesus"* (1 Tim 2:5 NLT). He is the ultimate Priest, but we also have the ministry of priesthood.

The priesthood had a threefold function. First, they sacrificed animals for the people, leading to the forgiveness of sins. Second, they witnessed to the people the works and glory of God. Third, they made intercession for individuals with their fasting and prayers.

As priests, one of our main functions is worshiping God. *"Therefore, let us offer through Jesus a continual sacrifice of praise to God, proclaiming our allegiance to His name"* (Heb. 13:15 NLT).

CONCLUSION

At one time, identifying a church was simple. It was a group of believers meeting to fellowship with Jesus, learn about Him, and carry out the Great Commission. That concept of the church was stretched when believers constructed a building and met under its roof. They called this structure "a church," and in its rooms they carried out the ministry of a church. As adequate as that definition was, it didn't quite include all the meanings of the New Testament church.

Today, there are new ways to compose a church:

1. *The business model church.* I came across this type of church in Vancouver, Canada. A local church was built on a business model, and board members each owned stock in the church. The church was

organized to own the property and rent its facilities during the five days of the work week; that would cover all the costs of the building and equipment. At the same time, the church paid taxes on its profits and other taxable income. The church had free use of the facilities on Sunday. That was foreign to my thinking as a citizen of the United States, but according to the laws of Canada, it was acceptable.

2. *The media church.* Some churches are made up of either a radio or television audience and now in modern times, a social media audience. While these church entities do not meet geographically, they come together in purpose, nature, limited fellowship, and worship.

Zion Fellowship of the greater McKinney, Texas, area has over 30,000 members whom Pastor Chuck Pierce calls "other sheep not of this fold." The pastor intentionally recruits Christians through an aggressive television and online ministry. These members come under the watch care of the fellowship after they go through a membership class online. They share the Lord's Table together. Those away from the home location partake of the cup and bread at the same time, watching the believers in McKinney do the same. Likewise with baptism, people are baptized in Jacuzzis, bathtubs, swimming pools, and/or any place where there is "much water."

The degree of interaction and connection among media churches varies. While many in traditional churches gather in a face-to-face relationship, does Scripture prohibit an assembly of people who gather through media from calling themselves church? If they assemble by other means rather than physically or geographically, can they be called "a church"?

3. *The multisite church.* This is one church located in several locations and held together by the sermons of the mother church that may be projected to satellite locations, by tape, television, or Internet. The senior pastor of the mother church gives direction to all pastors

at each satellite location, and the church is held together by shared *vision* and *values*. The secondary locations are also called "video venues" or "satellite campuses."

4. *The house church.* Technically, a house church is a local church that meets in a home; however, some churches also meet in restaurants, laundromats, or other public places. It is called a "house church" because it is smaller than an institutional church, does not own a physical structure, and does not have the usual characteristics of organizational assemblies.

I visited a house church in Lynchburg, Virginia, on a Sunday morning where three men got together and listened to an audio tape of a sermon from a preacher representing an extreme right-wing version of fundamental Christianity and American politics. It didn't seem like a church to me as far as purpose and/or makeup. This seemed more like a reactionary group that called itself a church.

In the United States, there are some organized 501(c)(3) entities that first incorporated themselves as nonprofit religious entities. Some of these seem to be an attempt to channel money for humanitarian or religious purposes as a tax write-off as allowed by United States income tax laws.

Is a church known by its intent or by its purpose? Just because a group of believers calls themselves a church does not necessarily mean they are a church. God may bless them, use them, and even manifest His presence in them, but they might not be a church.

However, groups that are identified as a church in the New Testament became a model for ministry and were blessed when God manifested Himself in them.

Remember, the Bible is not a written theology book. There are many expressions of systematic theology written by men such as John Calvin, Charles Hodge, James Strong, and Lewis Sperry Chafer.

Also, there are corporate expressions of systematic theology as in the Nicene Creed, the Chalcedonian Creed, the Westminster Confession of Faith, and the New Hampshire Statement of Faith (used by early Baptists in America). In these works, there are both limitations and extensions of the church's ministry.

God didn't write a theological textbook; rather, the Scriptures are a reflection of how people communicated to God, worshiped God, and served Him. We understand the church in this reflection.

On the other hand, the Scriptures are a revelation of the nature and purpose of God, so from the Bible we know Him better and understand what the church ought to be and how it should minister.

Perhaps God understood that when His people are assembled together—in a church—that assembly would look different in different cultures. It would feel different when dominated by different age groups. God creates every person differently, but at the same time, He uses each person. Perhaps God wanted His churches to be different in feeling, expression, and emphasis, yet cut from the same pattern so each have similar characteristics.

The church is like a person, and God created people to be both independent and dependent. They are independent before God and stand alone in accountability to God. That means they answer only to God. But yet each person is dependent on other people for social life, mental growth, emotional happiness, and spiritual fellowship. These two forces operate against each other at times and at other times cooperate with each other.

The independence of man says he must direct his own life and be responsible for everything he does. But in his isolation, he realizes that he finds meaning and purpose in connection with other people. Because what he wants and needs cannot be acquired by himself. He depends on other people to help him find food, clothing, shelter, and emotional happiness.

So, just as a person is independent, so every local church as a body is independent of all other churches and must find its doctrinal stability in the Word of God. It finds its practice of Christian living from God and in the final analysis will be accountable to God alone. But every church must relate to all other churches in mutual fellowship and mutual support. Every church must demonstrate that they are one in Christ with other churches and that every believer is one with all other believers. They must be one in purpose, one in passion, and one in shared values.

All believers can't be in one church, but each believer can be loyal to his/her church, serve in that church, and from that church reach out to complete the Great Commission.

CHAPTER 11

ANSWERS TO QUESTIONS ABOUT CHURCH PLANTING

Jesus first introduced the church with the statement *"...I will build My church..."* (Matt. 16:18 NLT). Notice He said that He would do it; He did not command us to plant a church or tell us how to plant a church or even ask if we could plant a church.

The questions of how, when, and where are not answered in Scripture. But this chapter will attempt to deal with some of those questions.

We can begin to see answers by studying the way the early church did it. When believers were persecuted in Jerusalem, many left and planted a church in Samaria and Antioch (see Acts 8:4-5). First, Philip, a deacon in the church, left and went down to Samaria and began preaching to them. Great revival broke out, and there were many saved, along with a demonstration of many miracles, including healings. After they were converted, they were baptized. Among the first people mentioned was Simon: *"Simon himself believed and was baptized..."* (Acts 8:13 NLT). He was probably not the first baptized but the first identified.

This was new territory so the church in Jerusalem sent a delegation to recognize or officially endorse the effort:

> *When the apostles in Jerusalem heard that the people of Samaria had accepted God's message, they sent Peter and John there. As soon as they arrived, they prayed for these new believers to receive the Holy Spirit. The Holy Spirit had not yet come upon any of them, for they had only been baptized in the name of the Lord Jesus. Then Peter and John laid their hands upon these believers, and they received the Holy Spirit* (Acts 8:14-17 NLT).

The fact that Peter and John came down from Jerusalem doesn't mean they needed authority from the mother church; it suggests that they came for further teaching and prayer. They wanted to be sure that new believers were walking in the fullness and power of the Holy Spirit.

Persecution also scattered Christians, who left Jerusalem and went to Antioch. *"Meanwhile, the believers who had been scattered during the persecution after Stephen's death traveled as far as Phoenicia, Cyprus, and Antioch of Syria"* (Acts 11:19 NLT). That new church in Antioch also had revival: *"The power of the Lord was with them, and a large number of these Gentiles believed and turned to the Lord"* (Acts 11:21 NLT).

This time, Jerusalem didn't send Peter and John, but rather Barnabas was sent to nurture the work in Antioch: *"...they sent Barnabas to Antioch. When he arrived and saw this evidence of God's blessing, he was filled with joy, and he encouraged the believers to stay true to the Lord"* (Acts 11:22-23 NLT).

When we look at how the church in Samaria and Antioch developed, we begin to see some patterns of how new churches would be planted, and from the stories we can conclude certain church planting principles.

1. *Should a man begin a church in his hometown?* There is a feeling among many that you cannot be a successful church planter in your own hometown. It comes from the words of Jesus: "*...a prophet is not honored in his own hometown*" (John 4:44 NLT). This idea is reiterated in the other Gospels. Many have felt that a pastor or church planter must leave his people and town to go minister elsewhere.

However, Jesus returned to His hometown, Nazarene, to minister to them (see Luke 4:16). Also, when Jesus talked about one's hometown, it did not mention a successful ministry there, but only that the minister would be "without honor." Perhaps that's because people remember a pastor's immaturity or mistakes as a young Christian. So, some teach that a church planter can't return home.

Another point to remember: Barnabas went to Cyprus, his home, to plant a church when he first left Antioch. Then Paul went back to his home in Tarsus after he began his ministry. So did the disciples of Jesus.

In 1969, when I wrote the book *The Ten Largest Sunday Schools and What Makes Them Grow*, I noted that those who built the largest churches in America had settled down in their home area and invested a lifetime of ministry.[1] Jerry Falwell did that, Harold Henninger did that, and so did some of the other pastors.

Perhaps a church planter's natural love for his home city and people can be used of God, motivating him to return to his home area. God uses his natural love of home as a burden to reach lost people in that area. And modern examples of this are Yonggi Cho, who settled in South Korea, and Andy Stanley, who settled in the north side of Atlanta where he was raised.

2. *What should be the polity of a new church?* The New Testament does not write out a doctrinal statement for new churches or existing churches. Apparently, the standard was *"teaching them to obey all things I* [Jesus] *have taught"* (Matt. 28:20 ELT). Perhaps the polity for a new church is found in the teachings of Jesus.

A church planter should not start off by trying to give a complete presentation of his doctrinal statement, nor should he try to be inoffensive by hiding what he believes. He may think this will attract new members. They may come for a while but will probably leave when they find out the "cost" of following Jesus. Rather, the church planter should challenge all to follow Jesus because salvation is in Him. Also, He is the church, and when they follow Jesus, they will do it in His church. Remember what was said earlier: Jesus attracts, but doctrine divides. Let Jesus be the theme of a new church.

First, exalt the preeminence of Jesus Christ as the divine Lord and Savior. Jesus Christ was fully God at all times and fully man in His birth, growth, and death. Anything less than the deity and humanity of Jesus Christ is a dangerous presupposition for a new church.

Second, always point people to the Bible as the ultimate authority. It is sufficient for their salvation and for the daily life of believers. The Bible will tell them all they need to know about God, salvation, sin (and how to have victory over it), and the abundant Christian life.

Third, the new church must challenge everyone to read, study, know, and interpret the Word of God for themselves.

Fourth, the Scriptures teach Christians to be good citizens, to be loyal to their government, to pay their taxes, and to pray for those in authority over themselves. The church planter should never seek governmental authority and/or financial support for his salary or for the new church.

Throughout history, there have been many state churches, for example, the Anglican Church in England and the Lutheran Church in Germany. Even some of the early American colonies were represented by one denominational church.

Fifth, do not accept anyone as a member of the church who is not born again or who is unwilling to follow Jesus Christ in all things. This will guarantee doctrinal purity and biblical power.

Sixth, a new church must be committed to the symbolic ordinances of believer's baptism and the Lord's Table. Both are in obedience to the commands of the Lord. The first symbol of salvation is baptism, and the symbol of continual fellowship with the Lord is partaking in the communion service regularly.

Seventh is the complete independence of the church but with interdependent fellowship with other churches of like faith and practice. A church gets its authority from God, and God directs every believer in the local church; and through their fellowship, service, and vote, they give direction to the church from God. We believe in the majority vote. "Let the majority have their way, but at all times let the minority have their say."[2]

But even as a church is independent from other churches, it always is dependent on God. It exercises interdependence in associated fellowship with other churches of like belief and like practice. As suggested, "The majority rule guarantees equal rights to all, and special privileges to none."[3] This concept of the freedom and obligation of church members was one of the motivating factors that led to the American Revolution and the establishment of the American Constitution, which gives freedom of speech and actions to all but also extends the obligations of citizenship to all.

Eighth, every church must commit itself to a worldwide missionary endeavor, evangelizing all and planting another church like itself that will reproduce itself and multiple other churches. This will fulfill the final command of Jesus.

Ninth, the church must believe in the imminent premillennial return of Christ in the air to gather believers to Himself and take them home to be with Him forever.

3.   *What type of authority should be followed in a church plant?* There are three types of church authority. First, there is a Presbyterian or representative governance of the church. The elders and/or deacons (that is, the church board) are the final human authority for the life and direction of the local church. However, they recognize that the final authority is with God and found in Scripture. The people/congregation elect elders and deacons, giving them church authority under God.

The second is an Episcopal church government whereby authority is invested in a godly leader who may be called pastor, bishop, or president. The church constitution recognizes that God gives him authority to lead the church by ministry and/or by decision-making. This authority is found in the Word of God.

Third is Congregational church government. Church authority rests in the congregation. As each member is filled by Christ and desires to please Christ, they give the church direction from the Lord Jesus. They get that direction from God Himself through the Scriptures. It is a church government of the people, for the people, and by the people. Every believer has an obligation to influence by counsel or direct vote in local church matters.

Look at examples of New Testament churches. Where was the authority? When Paul wrote to the Corinthian church, he was concerned about several issues in the church. Note what he did not do. Paul did not instruct elders or the pastor of the church to correct the problem. He appealed to the members of the church to solve the problems. It seems authority rested with the believer.

4. *What is the vision statement?* A vision statement is the application of the Great Commission in ministry to the community. It describes the future of the church and how its vision is carried out. See, for example, the vision statement of Rick Warren when he first planted Saddleback Church in Orange County, California.[4]

5. *How to choose a name for the church?* It is imperative that the correct name for the new church is chosen. It will outlast the present pastor and, in most occurrences, the members who helped start the church. Therefore, give the new church a name that will identify what the church will do and what it stands for. The new church name should speak of its strength. Is it a church for the community, or for fellowship among members, or for Bible teaching? A few churches call themselves "First Church," or "Neighborhood Church," or some other geographical designation, for example, "Central Church" and "Westside Church." Make sure your church name gives it a spiritual identity.

6. *Should the church have the name "Baptist"?* (Note that my convictions are not necessarily your convictions.) The name "Baptist" says the church is carrying out the Great Commission. The purpose of a church is to go everywhere and preach the Gospel to everyone, which will lead to baptism. Jesus said, *"Baptiz[e] them in the name of the Father and the Son and the Holy Spirit"* (Matt. 28:19). Since baptism is included in the command to go into all the world, why should it not be included in the church name?

When a church carries the name "Baptist," it tells the community that the most important thing about its function is salvation, that is, getting people saved, following Jesus Christ, and becoming a part of His church. That means the word "Baptist" makes evangelism more important than liturgy.

Also, since the name "Baptist" is usually associated with conservative Christians, that name means the church is committed to biblical inerrancy and preaching the death, burial, and resurrection of Jesus Christ.

Moreover, the name "Baptist" says that the church is committed to congregational authority. Obviously, the name "Presbyterian" means the church is committed to representative authority so that elders lead the church. Also, the name "Episcopal" means authority is given to the person in office, whether that authority is in a local pastorate or a superintendent/bishop over the churches. The name "Baptist" means the church is usually a church of the people, for the people, and by the people.

I remember reading a survey years ago that asked people, "What kind of church would you visit on a vacation?" Approximately 90 percent of the respondents said they would visit a Baptist church. That's good. But at the same time, the newspaper asked what church they would not visit. A different group of 90 percent said they would not attend a Baptist church. That survey reflects many different attitudes toward Baptists in the United States.

Many people have bad memories about a Baptist church, a Baptist church member, or a specific incident that happened at a Baptist church. Perhaps they were treated unfairly or went to a Baptist church that wasn't hospitable, or maybe they were disappointed in a Baptist church leader. Therefore, the name "Baptist" may present barriers to a large number of people who are not Christians.

Today, many people want to attend a church that doesn't have denominational or cultural barriers. They feel the church ought to be about Jesus Christ, not its religious heritage or its affiliation. Therefore, there are those who choose not to attend a Baptist church; they would probably not attend a Presbyterian church, a Methodist church, or any church with a denominational name.

Another survey showed that people are more likely to attend a church that identifies with their geographical location, such as Centerville Baptist Church (the name of a town), Westside Community Church, or Main Street Church (a specific street location).

Another reason to leave the name "Baptist" off is to make the congregation feel open and inviting to people. A church without a name or title may be better than one that suggests barriers or divisions. Dr. Jerry Falwell told Liberty University church planters, "Use the name Baptist, then determine to make the name good."[5]

7. *How shall finances be gathered to plant a church?* Sometimes it seems that the more financial help is given to a church, the less likely it is to grow. This could be compared to young people leaving home: sometimes the more money parents give their children, the less they will work for themselves. Could that be the case with church planting?

But at the same time, think of all that parents want to do and all they do correctly for their children. They invest in their children's education and college tuition knowing it will help them make a living when they get out of school. Most young people could not make it in the world if finances were not invested in them to prepare them for the time when they leave home.

So, let's look at the local church. The issue is not whether money is given to them or not; the issue is what investment can be made in them to begin a church successfully? Remember the principle of *division of labor*? People cannot do what God has reserved as His priority in ministry. On the other hand, God will not do what He has instructed people to do. Money represents more than finances; sometimes money represents the life of the mother church being poured into the satellite church, or it represents prayer support or sending workers to help in a new church.

8. *What kind of financial help should be given to a church plant and how much?* As stated above, finances can help in the planting and growth of a new church. However, if too much money is given, will the young church depend too much on the mother church? The mother church should give enough money so that the baby church can walk on its own feet, care for its own needs, and direct its own life.

Sometimes a weekly stipend from the mother church will help the new church in its early days of struggle. At other times, an offering can be taken at the mother church for the new church. Or individuals in the mother church can pledge to support the new church.

Also, there may be some gifts of land and other resources. One church planter from Liberty had a new car given to him when he went to Seattle, Washington, and another student had a car given to him when he went to Phoenix, Arizona.

Sometimes the mother church can make the down payment on the satellite church's first building. The down payment will get them in the building and operating on a sound financial basis until the satellite church is able to sustain monthly payments.

The indigenous principle for the church should be: "self-support-ing, self-governing, and self-propagating."[6] What does that mean? It means a new church must pay its own expenses, that is, be self-supporting. A new church should make decisions about its operations and destiny, that is, be self-governing. And a new church should evangelize its "Jerusalem" so that it is winning its members to Jesus Christ, that is, be self-propagating.

So what can be done? Perhaps it is better to give financial support to the church planter in the early days. That way, a church can pay for its own necessities, win souls to Christ, and direct its own destiny.

An established church can supply workers to help the new church get started. But if a new church depends on the labor of outside min-istries, then that church may struggle.

One last word about this: any established church should not consider itself too small to help support a new work financially. Nor should it consider itself too small to go out and send a team to reproduce another church.

9. *Should a church planter work to help support himself?* This is a question of tentmaking. Many church agencies have struggled with the issue of bivocational church planting (the church planter works to pay his personal expenses) as opposed to giving the church planter support from outside the new church.

It is generally agreed that the Apostle Paul worked as a tentmaker with Aquila and Priscilla. *"Paul lived and worked with them, for they were tentmakers just as he was"* (Acts 18:3 NLT). Paul worked in an occupation taught to him by his father. Normally, at a Bar Mitzvah, the father would proclaim, "He shall be a _____." The father declared that the son would have the same occupation as him. Therefore, it was assumed that Paul's father said, "Paul shall be a tentmaker."

Therefore, the question arises, why did Paul work? Obviously, work was his self-identity, so he did what was natural to him. Also, he may have begun working to provide for his physical needs. Remember, support had not reached him yet from Philippi. But also, Paul was an example to the new church because he suggested that every member should work as hard as he did.

And there is another reason. Perhaps Paul used his working hours in personal evangelism. He could have been witnessing about Christ and attempting to lead both workers and customers to Christ.

But on the other hand, perhaps Paul's work was a stumbling block. Leon Morris writes, "The Greeks despised all manual labour, thinking of it as fit only for slaves."[7]

Paul reminded the Corinthians to give financially to projects because he had not come to Corinth to make a living off of them or to receive money from them. He noted, *"And we labor, working with our own hands..."* (1 Cor. 4:12). Also, Paul told the Thessalonians, *"For ye remember, brethren, our labour and travail: for labouring night and day, because we would not be chargeable unto any of you, we preached unto you the gospel of God"* (1 Thess. 2:9 KJV).

The word for *labor* here is *kopiomen,* which means "hard work to the point of exhaustion." Perhaps this is the way Paul worked at Thessalonica. Why did he do that? *"Neither did we eat any man's bread for naught; but wrought with labour and travail night and day, that we might not be chargeable to any of you"* (2 Thess. 3:8 KJV). Paul's reasons for working were to remove any criticism regarding why he was preaching the Gospel. There is also another side of the argument: if Paul took money from these churches, he might have weakened their growth and advancement.

But let us quickly note that Paul worked physically only in certain cities. In other places such as Philippi, Paul did not work, but received money from them (see Phil. 4:16).

WHAT ARE THE ADVANTAGES OF MODERN TENTMAKING?

When a man works at his vocation, he is self-sufficient in his lifestyle. Both he and the church can prosper. But also, the church planter can meet people while employed who may be prospects for his church.

Also, the working tentmaker will know the pressures that his people feel, and he can better minister to them in his sermons and personal counsel.

In addition, by working the church planter becomes a testimony to the people of the church that they should work as diligently as he does.

Finally, no one can ever accuse the church planter of being lazy, and when he's finally supported full-time, they will have confidence that he will work in the church as diligently as he did in his tentmaking vocation.

1. *What are the implied dangers of tent making?* After working 40 hours a week, he will have less time to pray, read, and prepare his messages. He is also not available when people have emergencies such as funerals, accidents, etc.

Also, the working pastor will have little time to visit the sick in the hospital, or to give counsel to needy individuals. On the other side, when the pastor is working, he can delegate that responsibility to other people. Thus he trains a staff of people in ministry who will help him in basic ministry as they reach out to the unsaved.

But how can the working pastor give himself fully to both his secular work and his church plant? Note what James writes: *"Their loyalty is divided between God and the world, and they are unstable in everything they do"* (James 1:8 NLT).

One final note: tentmaking may be a hindrance to faith. Perhaps people just can't trust God to supply their needs. Instead of trusting God to supply financial needs, the church planter is trusting his ability to make money.

2. *Who can begin a church?* There are some small denominations that feel only a New Testament church can legitimately constitute another New Testament church. This position is sometimes called "landmarkism." The landmark position believes that a new group of people cannot begin administering baptism or serving the Lord's Table until they get authority from a duly constituted New Testament church. They believe authority passes from the mother church to a new church. This means an individual cannot start a church on his

own, nor can any interdenominational or interchurch agency plant a church. Only a legitimate church can plant another legitimate church.

But there is a problem. First, the argument requires temporal continuity. If every local church had to trace its authority back to a previous legitimate church, which traces its authority all the way back to John the Baptist, who baptized Jesus, what happens if there was a break? Is history reliable enough that we can trace today's churches back to New Testament churches?

But on the other side, there is another question: Could a group of people who get converted reading the Word of God start a church? Do they have to seek a legitimate church to give them authority?

Let's go back to the original question: Who can start a church? Jesus is the only agent who founded the church. Remember He said, *"...upon this rock I will build My church; and the gates of hell shall not prevail against it"* (Matt. 16:18 KJV). The church founded by Jesus is legitimate.

Because Jesus started the church, and because Jesus calls people to ministry, and because Jesus guides people to preach the Gospel to win souls, and because all new people must be baptized in the name of the Father, the Son, and the Holy Spirit, how can anyone say it is wrong to baptize a new believer after they get saved? When many new believers are baptized, are they not congregationalized into a new church?

In my lifetime, I've seen many young men leave Liberty University and other evangelical colleges/seminaries to go start successful New Testament churches. The success of these churches gives credibility to their ministry and tells me they have done the biblical thing.

These new congregations do not lack spiritual power because they were not developed by a mother church or an "authentic" church. And what is spiritual power? It is the presence of God in a church (see Matt. 28:20). It is the leadership of God in their programs, mission, and outreach. It is God's anointing on their preaching and teaching of His Word. It is the fruit when others are called out of that church to go into full-time service as pastors, church planters, teachers, and missionaries.

But at the same time, I've seen certain church planters from the landmark position begin a New Testament church that failed. If their position is the only anointed New Testament method and it failed, how can they justify the inconsistencies of their failure?

In summary, a mother church is not necessary to authenticate a New Testament church. However, this is one way that God does it and one way it works best.

CONCLUSION

These are only a few of the questions and answers about church planting. Remember, when a man and woman reproduce a child, they have completed what God predicted: *"and the two shall become one flesh..."* (Mark 10:8). God didn't answer all the questions about techniques to fertilize an egg, but God put love within the couple for each other. They just loved each other, and a baby was produced according to God's creative principles that He established in the beginning. In the same way, when a church planter loves God with all his heart and loves his "lost" neighbors with the same love, then a new church can be born. When that happens, we can say, "It was because of love."

CHAPTER 12

46 PRACTICAL STEPS TO PLANTING A CHURCH

Many of the following suggestions apply to Western churches and may not apply to new church plants in the Third World. However, each church planter must know his culture and local situation when planting a church. Should any of these practical suggestions apply, please use them. However, if some of these practical steps do not work in your situation, please understand there are differences in ethnic neighborhoods, cultural backgrounds, and the economic and social makeup of a community.

Most church planters do not realize how much is involved in getting a church started until they attempt it. Remember, a new church starts without a name, facilities, musical instruments, organizational framework, and perhaps not even an address.

1. *The church planter must see the church in his mind as he begins to plan, pray, and develop a strategy to plant a new congregation.* Remember,

you cannot achieve what you cannot conceive. Therefore, vision is imperative. God instructs, *"Where there is no vision, the people perish..."* (Prov. 29:18 KJV). So, the church must be large in the heart of the church planter long before it becomes large in the neighborhood.

Why is vision important? The first law of leadership dictates that when people buy into your vision, they buy into your leadership.

Al Henson went to Nashville, Tennessee, to plant a church. He fasted and prayed every Wednesday for a year before planting the church.

2. *Be sure of your calling and guidance from God.* You want the assurance that God is leading you. *"For as many as are led by the Spirit of God..."* (Rom. 8:14). If your church will succeed, you must be confident that God is leading you to plant a church.

WHAT IS THE CALL OF GOD?

- A burden (see Mal. 1:1; Hab. 1:1)
- A desire (see Jer. 20:9)
- Fruit/evidence God has called you (see John 15:16)

If you are going to plant a church, make sure you have a call from God. That begins with a burden from the Lord. This means, "I *must* plant this church."

But the call of God involves a second factor. You must have a great inner desire to do it. This means, "I want to plant a church more than anything in life." If the church planter is not excited about planting the church, there will be little excitement in the hearts of those who follow or listen to his presentation.

The third aspect is some fruit that God has used you in the past. The church planter should examine his past ministry experiences. Has God used you to win souls, or at least to teach and preach to make a difference in the lives of people? Has God used you to present the Gospel to family and friends?

Pastor Yonggi Cho told me to tell the church planters from Liberty University that they should not attempt to start a church until they have fasted and prayed for the new church for at least ten days.

3. *Be sure that your spouse is convinced that this is the will of God for you.* The most important ingredient in planting a church is faith, spiritual works, and support from your spouse. After the church planter faces pressure, frustration, and failure on the field, it would be difficult to come home to a nagging spouse, or at least one who undermines his confidence. He will need the support from his spouse so that they pray together, plan together, and even work together.

4. *Be ready to teach and preach the Bible.* The greatest enticement to get people to be part of a new church is preaching the Word of God. You must believe the message is from God and is the only hope for lost people. Effective preaching is the basis by which a new church is planted. If you place your trust in your organization, money, supporting church, or any other entity, your new church will not be successful.

I suggest that church planters have around six months of sermons prepared before they begin a new church. When the church begins, a church planter cannot give extensive time to sermon preparation. He can do that later in ministry. When I have taught the Gospel of John, I usually tell a young man who is going to plant a church to take my notes and preach through John. I say, "Don't just read my notes; make the message your own. John is the greatest book in the Bible and will get the greatest results in your preaching. Therefore, preach through John to the new church because people will see Jesus, be convinced of His Deity, and put their trust in Him."

Carl Baugh, who began Calvary Baptist Church in St. Louis, Missouri, said he preached his best sermons to new small crowds when he began his church. He did not want to hold his best sermons until he had larger crowds. If his smaller crowds did not believe and follow, he would never get a chance to preach to larger crowds.

5. *Know your ecclesiology.* Know the church, what constitutes a church, how people enter a church, and how people serve God through a church. Know how a church responds to challenges and develops vision. This is another way of saying "love the church"—even *"as Christ also loved the church, and gave himself for her"* (Eph. 5:25). You will find the church planter giving himself for the church that he plants.

6. *Accept only new members who profess faith in Jesus Christ and have been baptized.* Once you accept a person into your church who has not been baptized, you will never again be true to your commitment to God and your church. Once I led a man to Christ in a hospital in Lynchburg, Virginia; then I led his wife to Christ. She came to Thomas Road Baptist Church, and I baptized her on a Sunday morning. I asked Pastor Jerry Falwell, "The husband wants to join the church along with his wife, but physically he cannot leave the hospital and come to church to be baptized."

Falwell responded, "If I accept him as a member, I could never look another new convert in the face and honestly say, 'You must be baptized to join the church.'" So, we baptized the wife and voted her into the church, but not him. Then Falwell explained to the congregation, "If you are happy that her husband is saved and that he will support Jesus Christ and Thomas Road Baptist Church from a distance, shout, 'Amen.'" There was a loud "Amen!" The church extended fellowship and watch care to him until he died. He was buried in a full church ceremony, but the church remained true to its conviction.

7. *Set long-range goals but also short-range goals.* The formula for success can be summarized in four words: *plan, organize, execute,* and *control.*

Many church planters begin a church and honestly do not have a philosophy of ministry. I was organizing Central Baptist Church on Long Island, New York, for Russ Merrin, a Liberty University graduate. He asked me for advice about how to handle a certain problem.

"WWJD," I answered with a smile on my face.

He thought I meant, "What would Jesus do?" But I shook my head no.

"WWJD stands for 'What would Jerry do?'" I laughed at my odd reply. Then I explained, "Jerry Falwell was not God, and he was not a perfect model for ministry. But he had successfully built one of the ten largest churches in America. Use Jerry as your model—not because he is perfect, but because he has successfully faced problems and built a church. Let Jerry be your model in ministry."

As he faced problems and solved every crisis the way Jerry did, he would build his own model in ministry. Then as he grew in ministry and the church grew in outreach, he would develop his own strength.

8. *Find the right city/location for the new church.* Sometimes God calls a church planter to plant a church long before He leads him to a specific location. Rudy Holland grew up at Thomas Road Baptist Church and planned to go plant a church just as Jerry Falwell did. He experienced that calling on his life for several months. But God had not led him to a location.

Rudy was driving back to Lynchburg from Tennessee Temple School, where he was a student. A friend was driving the car. As they drove along Interstate 81 in the foothills of the Blue Ridge

Mountains, Rudy looked out at the sea of lights in the Roanoke, Virginia, valley. At that moment, he knew God was calling him to plant a church in Roanoke. Eventually, he planted a church called "Berean Baptist Church" that grew to over 1,000 in attendance.

a. The Bible states that Jesus *"set [His] face as a flint"* (Isa. 50:7 KJV). That means He was determined. The church planter should have that kind of determination to plant and build a local church.

b. The church planter must commit himself to planting a church and reject all other options. He is not planting a church until something else better comes along. He is not planting a church in hopes that some larger church will call him as pastor. He is planting a church because God has called him to do it.

c. The church planter should pray initially about a location and then daily for the guidance of the Holy Spirit to the location.

d. Wait for the Macedonian Call. It was during a dark night when the call came to Paul, *"Come over into Macedonia, and help us"* (Acts 16:9 KJV). Sometimes God speaks in the dark of the night as we wait on Him in prayer. That is what happened to Rudy Holland. Sometimes the Macedonian Call will come by a phone call, or letter, or a conversation with someone who points the church planter to a location and/or need for a church.

At other times, a location may be found through circumstances or by an open door (see 1 Cor. 16:9). God led Rudy Holland to plant a church in Roanoke when he saw the lights of the city one evening before him. God led Carl Godwin to plant a church in his hometown because of his natural love for the area. God led Jerry Falwell to plant Thomas Road Baptist Church in Lynchburg because he had been saved in a church in Lynchburg and a group of people were planning on starting a church there and needed a pastor.

e. Recognize that the calling to a location is similar to the calling of God for full-time service. Remember that the call of God is threefold: it is, first, a burden for an area; second, a desire to go to the area; and third, an evidence of fruit that God's call is upon your life.

This means that God will work in the heart of the church planter to focus his attention on a location so he eventually rules out all other locations. This is how he develops confidence that God has led them there and will use him there.

f. Talk to the people of God and ask them about the area—and not just to pastors, but lay people and those from the area as well. Local insight may be a tremendous help in guiding the church planter.

g. Usually the church planter should not go to an area that is already evangelized. If there is a large evangelistic church located there or many New Testament churches, the church planter should have doubts about God's leadership to that location. Because there are so many other needy places without churches, why would God lead the church planter to an area already saturated by the Gospel? So, God may lead a man to an area where there are churches, but the church planter should seek absolute certainty that this location is God's will.

h. Choose a place that has a large number of needy people. When new neighborhoods are going up in the United States, that means there are people without church relationships. Therefore, they would be open to attending a new church. But also new people in new neighborhoods usually have "little roots." According to statistics, people who are in transition are more open to the Gospel than those who have been settled in an area, a home, and a job; have neighbors; and are comfortable in a routine of life.

i. Go visit the area as soon as possible. Walk through the neighborhoods and begin looking for places where the new church might meet. Look for community institutions, for example, banks, schools, police stations, fire stations, stores, manufacturing plants, and any other institutions of stability. In other words, make sure that you know the area, and that is done by walking the sidewalks, driving the streets, and surveying who and what is there.

j. Use volunteers from a planting church to take a community survey to get basic information on the people who live there.

9. *Determine to go first class.* When churches begin, there is rarely enough money to do everything perfectly, but the pastor should determine to do everything as best as possible. The location, advertising, music, preaching, etc., ought to be the best that can be offered. The pastor should dress correctly. The facilities should be bright and clean. In everything, the church planter must strive for quality.

Jerry Bunch began Liberty Baptist Church in Orange County, California, by renting a conference room in a plush hotel. Instantaneously, the church had an image of excellence. If it had started in a storefront, it would have had an image of mediocrity. Bunch realized the important principle of "first seed reference," that is, a church will grow as it is planted. If you begin with a storefront mentality, you will attract people who expect that level of quality. But if you begin with a high standard, you will attract quality personnel. It is true that second-rate individuals will attend a quality church, but the reverse is probably not true. A quality individual will not attend a church in a "second-rate" building.

Some fundamentalists believe sophistication and revivalism cannot be mixed. At the first anniversary of Canyon Creek Baptist Church in North Dallas, Texas, a symphony orchestra dressed in tuxedos provided the music. Sophistication was everywhere apparent. But when the congregation joined in singing "Oh, How I Love Jesus," a revival spirit filled the tent. When sinners walked an old-fashioned sawdust trail, a mixture of "first-class music" and "spirituality" was evident.

10. *Have a positive attitude.* George Zarris planted Fox River Baptist Church in Aurora, Illinois, and felt lonely the first few weeks. But he testifies, "As I told everyone I was starting a church, I suddenly realized I was somebody—I was a child of the King. I was doing something no one else was doing. I was starting a church." That self-image supported him in his loneliness. Bill Monroe

posted motivational signs of success around his office to keep himself motivated. Jerry Falwell constantly reminded students at Liberty University to be power conscious, not problem conscious.

The pastor who constantly thinks he might fail will probably fail. Yet if God has called him, and if the Holy Spirit has led him, and if he has no unconfessed sin in his life, and if he has properly studied and prayed, he will succeed (see Phil. 4:13).

11. *Start a pastor-led church.* The secret that will make your church successful and different from other churches is your leadership. As is often said, "Everything rises or falls on leadership." Committee-run churches (those controlled by the deacons) rarely experience the growth of pastor-led churches. This is not a put-down of deacons. The word *deacon* means "servant." Every church needs servants as well as pastors (the word *pastor* means "shepherd").

As a matter of fact, a committee, or a board of deacons, has rarely planted a church. Because starting a church is such a gigantic step of faith, it is a step usually taken alone by the man or woman of God, not in concert with others. Therefore, leaders, not committees, usually start churches.

12. *Do not neglect your walk with God.* The ministry is one of the easiest places to backslide. It is possible to become so involved in the ministry you can forget its spiritual basis. Al Henson prayed daily for Nashville three years before he started Lighthouse Baptist Church. Jeff Winstead and his wife, Audrey, fasted and prayed one day per week for a year before starting Harvest Baptist Church in Hagerstown, Maryland. Jerry Falwell preached a sermon exhorting preachers to pray daily for love—love for people, love for God, and love for family. As a result, many pastors have been motivated to include these three items on their daily prayer list.

13. *Commit yourself to share the Gospel with individuals.* A church must be built through relationship evangelism. When a church planter starts from scratch, he must win all of his church members. It is possible to plant a new church from a split off of another church or by adding disgruntled members from surrounding churches. But if the new church is not winning souls to Christ, it will eventually experience problems. The secret to well-rounded growth in all areas is evangelism. The secret to building a church to 1,000 members is to use the same principles General Motors uses to make a million cars. They build them one at a time. A great church will be built as one soul is won, one at a time.

14. *Have biblical standards for workers.* One temptation in starting a church is to use anyone until someone better comes along. But this is building your foundation on the sand rather than a rock. Have biblical standards for workers in the church. Some young church planters think they can use anyone in a new church with a view of "preaching hard" in the future and raising standards.

The "first seed reference" of the church is predictive of its continuing ministry. It is almost impossible to overcome weaknesses built into a new church.

One church planter noted, "I taught all the teenagers and adults in one Sunday school class while my wife taught all the children in one other Sunday school class." He went on to explain he would rather have fewer classes and biblical workers than add Sunday school classes that had to be taught by carnal workers. Not only should a church planter do this, but he should also tell his people why. Challenge the congregation to (1) pray for workers, (2) qualify themselves as workers, and (3) have confidence in the pastor because he knows what he is doing. This way the congregation will not think the pastor is trying to keep all the jobs to himself.

15. *Learn from great men.* Greatness in the ministry is developed by associating and learning from other great leaders. I have often called this the "hot poker" philosophy. The poker gets hot as it is placed in the burning coals. The church planter will grow in enthusiasm and skill as he learns from those who are doing it. Great leaders will teach you to lead confidently and to preach enthusiastically. They can teach you how to look after details and organization, plus give you a pioneering spirit.

Someone has said that the difference between what you are today and what you will be five years from now is the people you meet and the books you read. Carl Godwin graduated from a Nazarene college but planted an independent church after studying the ministry of Jerry Falwell. He testified that many taught him how to build a church, but Jerry challenged him to do it. Jim Singleton planted a church after fellowshipping with great men like John R. Rice. Bill Monroe relied on the advice of Greg Dixon, pastor of Indianapolis Baptist Temple, and Cecil Hodges, pastor of Bible Baptist Church in Savannah, Georgia. The successful church planter is one willing to continue learning from great men.

Many successful church planters have told other men just starting to "phone me." The new church planter needs constant encouragement, and when he faces trouble, he needs someone to whom he can go for counsel.

Greatness in the ministry is developed by associating and learning from other great men. G.B. Vick, pastor of Temple Baptist Church in Detroit, Michigan, taught the students at Baptist Bible College in Springfield, Missouri, that great men build great churches, but average men build average churches.

HOT POKER

Meet great men
Read great books
Attend great events
Visit great locations

16. *Learn the biblical use of money.* The use of money in starting a church is more important than anything else, except the use of people. In the final analysis, a leader's attitude toward people will influence the way he handles finances. The Florence Baptist Temple has experienced phenomenal growth for many reasons. One of the church's strengths is Pastor Bill Monroe's attitude toward money. He sees that there are two basic philosophies in church financing. First, there is management by assets. Many church leaders feel that as long as assets are greater than liabilities, a church can expand through deficit financing. These leaders have gone into excessive bond programs, purchasing more assets (building, property, buses, television equipment) but always keeping their total debt under their total worth. As a result, their church has a good financial record on paper, but there is one problem. Many of these churches struggle with weekly income to pay off their indebtedness. Some have gotten into financial trouble, having to sell off assets or face the embarrassment of not being able to pay their debts.

The second philosophy is financing by cash flow. This approach simply controls the spending so that a church will not obligate itself for more resources or loans than its weekly offerings can presently cover. When a church does this, it can pay all of its operating expenses. This simple philosophy dictates that a church must have more cash incoming than outgoing.

Monroe has built his church on cash flow. This has resulted in large facilities, respect from the financial community, confidence of the congregation, and a sound basis on which to plan future growth.

17. *Don't badger the people for extra money.* As a church planter, teach people the New Testament principle of tithing and motivate everyone to tithe. Do not take many extra offerings. Material possessions should always be secondary in the Lord's work, but some churches have made it primary. A person's relationship to Jesus Christ is the most important ministry of a church. When a man loves God, he will give out of obedience and love.

18. *Keep finances open.* Give a regular financial report to the congregation in which all expenses are listed and explained to the congregation. However, staff salaries should not be listed individually. It is not right to reveal a staff member's salary any more than it is to reveal what each member of the church makes. When people have a question about the finances, approach the topic and answer the question honestly.

19. *Get an audited statement the first year.* The business community will have great respect for a church that has a certified public accounting firm issue an annual audited statement. That means an examination is made to determine the church's integrity and the way it handles finances. As a result, the people give with confidence because they know an outside authority places its "stamp of approval" on finances.

Many people may not have confidence in a new church, or even its pastor. Therefore, get an audited statement at the end of the first year. To get this accomplished, a CPA will have to be contracted during the first year of operations. When the statement is received, take it to the banker and other businesses associated with the church. It will give them confidence in the new church and will give credibility when going for a loan.

A church planter should seek financial advice from the business community. Listen to accountants, but going against an accountant is a financial risk. An accountant will be right more times than financial advice from fellow pastors or other interested friends.

20. *Have a stewardship campaign the first year.* Stewardship is defined as properly managing one's time, talent, and treasure to the glory of God. A stewardship series is dedicated to teaching stewardship, not asking for money, but instructing how each person should handle their money according to God's standards. Sunday school lessons as well as every sermon should emphasize managing money for God.[1] During the campaign, testimonies are given by laymen on how God has blessed them. During the stewardship campaign, an audited report is given to every member along with a budget for the coming year. Then ask each member to commit themselves financially to a total lifestyle of stewardship. Plan a stewardship banquet with a good program with a well-known speaker invited to bring the stewardship message. Prior to the banquet, dedicate the month to emphasizing stewardship. Every Sunday school lesson as well as every sermon emphasizes managing money for the glory of God. Testimonies are given by laymen on how God has blessed them because they have tithed.

At the stewardship banquet, an audited report is given to every member, along with a budget for the coming year. The people are presented with what they have done in the previous year and what they can do through tithing. Let them know their tithing has resulted in buildings, equipment, property, and souls who have been saved because they have given sacrificially.

21. *Expect a congregation to tithe from the first Sunday the church is planted, and a new Christian should tithe when they are first saved.* Many young church planters are reluctant to press people to tithe, thinking

that pressure will scare off potential members. Unless a church is started with its members being aware of their financial obligation to God, the church will always have money problems. If new members are with the church in money, new members are with the church in every other area of ministry.

Teach people the meaning of money. Money is life. A man sacrifices his strength or time to get a paycheck. So, when a member gives money to a church, they are giving their strength or life back to God when they drop money in the offering plate. Therefore, giving is the highest form of worship because we are giving ourselves back to God.

22. *Keep excellent financial records.* When the church first begins, install a bookkeeping system throughout the church. A new church needs a complete system of books so the church will have accurate records. Bill Monroe advises a young pastor to hire a bookkeeper as soon as you can afford one. Monroe gets a financial report every Monday morning. He is never in the dark about the financial condition of the church.

23. *Have cash on hand to operate for four weeks.* Churches should have cash on hand to operate on a business-like basis. Most of the churches that operate on cash flow have finances spread across several accounts so that if the money does not come in, the church's ministry is not threatened, nor will they lose their testimony by not being able to pay their bills. This is quite the opposite of some churches that extend themselves financially so that the church planter runs to the back of the auditorium every Sunday to see if the offering is large enough to cover the checks issued last Friday. Obviously, a new church cannot have four weeks of cash on hand as a reserve. But even a new church can keep some on hand for last-minute emergencies.

24. *Survey the town.* When Dr. David Stauffer received his PhD from seminary, he wanted to start a church. He chose St. Louis

because it was one of the top 10 metropolitan areas in the nation, and he had heard there had never been a great growing church in the area. He arrived in town pulling all his furniture on a rental trailer. He stayed in a motel for a week trying to find a place to start the Calvary Christian Temple. He created an urban chart projecting future density, traffic patterns, population growth, trying to find a neighborhood that would cover the span from the upper to lower classes. He ultimately bought seven and a half acres in the center of four expressways in south St. Louis County.

The church planter should obtain the best city map available and mark all churches on the map, not forgetting those which are operating in homes, rented buildings, or have projected building plans.

George Zarris drove to the Chicago area looking for a place to start a church. He was looking for (1) a high-population area, (2) an area that did not have a growing church, (3) an area where land was available for future expansion, and (4) a place where they could rent a building or auditorium. Steve Frankenberger flew Zarris over the city of Aurora in his plane. They could not tell much from the air, but in that small plane George determined that Aurora was the area. Previously, he had been told that Fox River Valley would be the center of the population of the state of Illinois. The Sunday *Chicago Tribune* supported the decision with an article on the front page discussing a multi-million dollar shopping center in Aurora.

In larger cities, statistical information can be gathered from a US Census Report, the city librarian, the city engineer's office, or the local building inspector. The number of births in the area can be obtained by checking with the Public Health Department. The US Census will reveal the age-group distribution. The principals of schools can give the percentage of children who are Protestant, Jewish, or Catholic. If the area is not completely built up, local builders can help estimate how many houses will eventually be built in the area and what demand will be made for new houses. This information can also be obtained from city planners, building permit offices, and realtors.

After you have discovered the number of houses or dwelling units in the area, determine the average number of people in the area using the formula of 3.6 persons in each dwelling unit.

Some denominations maintain that a religious survey should be taken to discover church membership before a new church is considered for an area. However, church membership has no bearing on a person's relationship to God. Church planters go to a city under the leadership of the Holy Spirit and begin knocking on doors and winning people to Jesus Christ.

Some feel a new church should not be started with less than 100 families. However, some church planters have started with only one family. Some men have begun holding services with only their wives present. The eye of faith is sometimes greater than the mind of reason. Men have gone into a community to start a church under the leadership of God knowing He would bless and people would come to the new endeavor.

The Jews in biblical times began synagogues when 12 heads of families could reach an agreement to start a new congregation. This is a more realistic consideration for evangelical churches today.

Not every neighborhood is conducive to starting a church. It is more difficult to start a church in an old established neighborhood than in a new suburban development. Whereas settled residents tend to have their membership in an old church, mobile families in new neighborhoods are prospects for membership in new churches. Therefore, a growing neighborhood or a transient neighborhood provides a better opportunity for succeeding than an old neighborhood. Those who are mobile are eager to (1) find new friends, (2) establish new patterns of life, and (3) adapt to a neighborhood.

Mobile families suffer some culture shock. (Because of a disorientation to life around them, they search for stability. A church meets their existential need.) When a person goes through geographical mobility, he also undergoes psychological mobility. Hence, he is a candidate for the Gospel. Having been cut off from the stability of the past, he has a greater need to connect with people.

Some might criticize the principle of building a church in a neighborhood that is most conducive to the Gospel. Yet, Jesus commanded His disciples to go into a new city, and if they were not received, to shake the dust off their sandals (see Matt. 10:14). Jesus was advocating that His disciples should endeavor to win those who are most receptive to the Gospel and not invest as much time on those who would not receive it. (However, He did not advocate avoiding those who were not receptive.)

If a church planter is seeking a location, he might spend more energy in a neutral suburb than a Jewish neighborhood, knowing that he would probably win more to the Lord in one than the other. This does not mean he should never present the Gospel to the Jews. The Bible teaches that Christ died for all and that *"all have sinned and fall short of the glory of God"* (see John 3:16; Rom. 3:23). Therefore, he should attempt to win all. But the greatest investment of his energies should be given to those who are most receptive to the Gospel.

Many times, those beginning new churches become "star-struck" wanting to minister to the upper class or elite. However, money is often an insulation against the needs of life. It is hard for a rich man to enter the Kingdom (see Matt. 19:23-24)—*hard*, but not impossible. At the same time, the poor are faced daily with the ultimate necessities of life. Hence, they have a greater dependence on God's work in their life. Often the poor will turn to Christ where the rich have a social snobbery and intellectual independence. A new church should minister among those most responsive to the Gospel. But it should not exclude the rich or aim only at the poor.

25. Choose a good name for the church. The name of the church will outlast the church planter in most cases. So, the choice of a new name is of utmost importance. Many urge church planters to "say what you want to do" with your name. By this they mean that the name should identify the church's vision. When church planter Doug Porter named his church Valley City Baptist Church (Dundas, Ontario), he indicated a desire to reach beyond the town of Dundas into the other communities of the greater Hamilton Valley. Jerry Falwell advised pastoral students at Liberty University not to follow his example in naming a church after a street address. Thomas Road Baptist Church has outgrown its Thomas Road address, but the name was not changed when the church moved to Liberty Mountain.

The name should also identify the nature of the church, though some might question whether you should use the word "Baptist" in a church name. For more on this, see Chapter 11.

CHOOSING A CHURCH NAME

Spiritual identity
Geographical identity
Reflective of the church's aim

The following are some examples of church names that speak to their vision and nature:

a. Central Baptist Church in Milwaukee, Wisconsin, because it was central to the city.

b. Tri-Cities Baptist Church in Gladstone, Oregon, because it had a ministry to the three major cities in South Portland.

c. New Life Baptist Church in Harrisburg, Pennsylvania, because the church offered new life in Christ.

d. Shenandoah Valley Baptist Church in Winchester, Virginia. Although not located immediately in Winchester, it has a ministry to all in the north valley.

e. Calvary Heights Baptist Temple in St. Louis, Missouri, because the church is on a hill and because Calvary is the foundation of Christianity.

f. Liberty Baptist Church in Irvine, California, because the Gospel frees a man and because the pastor wanted to identify with Dr. Jerry Falwell.

g. Twin Cities Baptist Church because the church was located between St. Paul and Minneapolis, Minnesota, and wanted to minister to both cities.

26. *Get a local address.* As soon as you know where you will start the church, establish a local address. Most church planters will open a post office box and have people send mail there. Some have used a post office box for months before the church was actually begun. A local address is needed to incorporate, open a bank account, etc., and will identify the church in the neighborhood.

27. *Receive money up to six months before the church begins.* As soon as the new church's city, name, and approximate date of beginning is known, the church planter should begin receiving money into the checking account. There may be some people in the area who have been praying for the new church who will give to the project. The church planter will have parents, relatives, and friends who pray for him. They may want to make financial gifts to the new church. Also, the church planter may want to make personal gifts to the new

church. Some even begin to divert their tithe from the mother church to the new church plant before arriving at the location.

Some of the greatest expenses for starting a new church come in the first months—moving, rent deposit on an apartment/building, printing, advertisement, etc. Therefore, the church planter should prepare a realistic budget for the first month's expectations and begin raising money to meet the need.

28. *Receipt all money.* The church planter will need to secure a receipt book that has the name of the church printed on the receipt, plus a sequence of numbers. Each gift must be recorded and a receipt issued. These records become a part of the new church's financial books. When the church is actually chartered, individual receipts will not be given on a weekly basis, but like other churches, it will issue a receipt at the end of the financial year. All gifts should be posted in a receipt journal.

29. *Plan a three-month budget.* The church planter will have to approximate all the expenses incurred in the first 90 days and make this a prayer goal. This becomes a realistic prayer challenge to share with churches and friends.

Preparing a budget for a nonexistent ministry is difficult but necessary. A budget is necessary for good financial management. Money is ministry. The way one handles the money is the way one handles the ministry. The following simple rules will help the young preacher starting out.

- Do not spend more money than you take in.
- Income should increase in proportion to membership.
- Always know how much money you have in all accounts.
- Keep good credit in the community and pay all bills on time.

When preparing the first budget, there are certain things to remember. First, include your moving expenses. The cost of moving is great regardless of how you do it. Also, the cost of housing should be considered. In the long run, buying your own home is cheaper than renting. When considering your personal budget, remember to include everything. Pastors are entitled to certain tax breaks with regard to housing, car allowance, and insurance. Keep these in mind as you prepare your personal budget.

1. Moving expenses (trailer rental, travel, meals, incidentals)	$
2. Deposit, rent, phone, utilities, etc.	$
3. Home rent for 90 days	$
4. Church rent for 90 days	$
5. Printing of Brochures	$
6. Postage	$
7. Advertisement	$
8. Salary	$
9. Utilities	$
90 Day Total	$
Needed per month	$

After the church planter sees the expenses of starting a church, he may want to quit. Perhaps no other reason has killed new churches more than a lack of financial planning. If the church planter can realistically see the cost and continue with his plans, then maybe this is an indicator that God is calling him.

30. *Raise financial support*. Just as the foreign missionary must raise his support before going to the field, so must the church planter also. The one exception is that the church planter will soon pastor a church that is self-supporting. Most church planters ask for financial support for six months to one year. Many potential givers are willing to take on a short-term responsibility for church planting but resist a life-long obligation.

Some church planters send out letters asking for money from friends. While it may not work well for all, some money received from this source was all the salary some church planters had received when starting the church.

Also, many pastors are eager to help church planters start churches. Several fellowships exist primarily to raise funds for new churches.

a. Send prayer letters to relatives and friends of the church planter. A brochure of the new work should be enclosed.

b. Solicit like faith churches for monthly support, or for the opportunity to make a presentation so that the church can give a one-time offering.

c. Some church planters schedule their prayer meetings on another night than Wednesday so that during the first few months they can travel to other churches to raise support.

d. If the church planter is leaving school, his friends may pledge financial support.

e. The home church or sponsoring church may provide monthly support or other support such as hymn-books, printing, musical instruments, amplifications, office equipment, etc.

f. A local fellowship of churches/pastors may offer to support the church planter.

31. *Begin gathering friends in the area.* When a church planter returns to his hometown, he will have a number of prospects among his old friends, relatives, etc. Upon returning to Lincoln, Nebraska, Carl Godwin got out his high school annual, *The Link*, and put his old high school buddies on his mailing list. As he began visiting former friends, some received the Lord. These people encouraged Godwin to go on with plans to begin the church. Prospects include anyone who is not attending a church but could and should attend your church. Some church planters have used the mailing lists of radio/television ministries. The first prospect may come from the other side of town from where the new ministry is located. Get names of prospects—find every available person, considering the following:

a. Addresses of friends and relatives

b. Newcomer lists

c. Former high school acquaintances (if pastor is returning to hometown)

d. Names of unchurched friends given by people in other churches

e. Community canvases

f. Door-to-door visitation

g. A phone response on mailings and other advertisements

h. Names of other potential members from those who attend "get acquainted" meetings.

32. *Use postal mail or e-mail.* Every time you meet someone who is interested in the new church, put his/her name on your mailing list. First, send each prospect an e-mail or letter inviting him/her to the

church. Include a brochure. Then begin sending a regular newsletter to each prospect with information about the new church.

You will not be able to see everyone on a regular basis, but your newsletter can go into every home telling people what God is doing in the new church. Do not use the newsletter to preach. Share the excitement of the work, and they may get excited.

33. *Saturate the community.* Use every available means to reach every available person at every available time. Announce the beginning of the church over television, radio, billboards, newspapers, buses, etc.

THINGS TO PLACE IN THE NEWSLETTER

1. Attendance (compare, so growth can be seen)
2. Offerings (show accumulation of offerings, so strengths can be seen)
3. Conversions
4. New items purchased
5. New aspects of the ministry
6. Have special days and promote them
7. Share goals and dreams

34. *Set ministry goals.* Most successful church planters set short-, medium-, and long-range goals. Generally, these goals aid in establishing direction and measuring progress. Some church planters set goals of how many members they should have at the end of the first year. Such an attendance objective will drive them to work diligently. Others know they will work with every ounce of strength. They do not need attendance goals.

1. Visits made

GOALS FOR A NEW CHURCH
2. Prospects on mailing list
3. Number in first (launch) service
4. Number of conversions
5. Number of charter members
6. 100 in the worship service
7. Number baptized at first baptismal service
8. Offering to reach $10 per attendee

35. *Get a temporary church sign outside.* Even if the only sign you can use is a portable sign, a well-painted sign is still a good advertising tool. It is better to have a permanent sign posted at your meeting place. Be sure to include the church's name, times of services, and a phone number for further information. Some churches use large sandwich boards in front of rented facilities.

36. *Post a sign behind the pulpit to direct attention to the purpose of the new church.* When guests come into your building, have a large sign with the logo and motto that identifies the church and pastor. A public school room or motel auditorium can be cold and indifferent. The church needs something to help the people focus their attention on the Lord Jesus Christ and the new church that is being formed.

37. *Print and distribute brochures and fliers.* Get brochures and fliers printed immediately. They should include information on the pastor, the vision statement or purpose statement, and the type of program the church will offer. Order early because printing requires time. A letter could be included with the flier. The old adage is still true: "You never get a second opportunity to make a first good impression." The brochure should be first-rate because prospects will judge the new church by their first impression. And their first

impression will be gleaned from a brochure. Prospects will not have a church building to tell them what type of church the new one will be; there has not been a church service by which they will make a judgment. So make the brochure colorful and exciting yet informative.

FIRST BROCHURE

1. Name of the church
2. Basic information: location, time, place
3. Brief statement of purpose
4. Pastor's name and picture
5. Pastor's accomplishments and education—to show church is not a "fly-by-night" idea
6. Services of church: nursery, children and youth programs, etc.
7. Plans—immediate and long range. People must be able to identify with pastor's vision
8. Credibility—letter from sponsoring church or other well-known minister and/or acknowledgment of support by a group of churches or denominations

---

38. *Hold "Get Acquainted" meetings.* Hold two or three meetings before beginning the church. Visit the entire neighborhood to invite people to these meetings. At the meeting, the church planter should present his vision to the people in a very friendly way. The Gospel can be presented, but there is no pressure to "walk the aisle." Most pastors who use this approach will gather a nucleus of interested people. These people may be from a dead church or completely unattached to a church. The main thing to do in these meetings is to share the burden and vision. Some people in dead churches may want the exact type of church that the church planter is proposing. Also, by not conflicting with regular church meetings, the prospect is not forced to make an attendance choice against his present church.

39. *Do not publicly attack other pastors and churches.* As soon as you begin the church, there will be those who disagree with the new church. Liberal churches will oppose its theology and fundamental churches will disagree that a need exists and may judge the church planter's motives in starting a church.

Some will be jealous of the new church's aggressiveness; others will be turned off thinking it is an outward show. Some may publicly criticize a new church. Remember, every time they criticize its ministry, they advertise its ministry. They may motivate some to come and see what the new church is all about. When a pastor attacks a new church from his pulpit, another pastor will think to himself, "How foolish. Since he's not doing anything, he is telling dissatisfied Christians that we are doing something."

The purpose of the new church is not to correct the other churches, and you cannot do it even if you tried. Also, it is not one church's duty to correct or improve another, for this seldom helps and always hurts the attacking church. The church planter should resist the temptation to fight fire with fire. He only has 24 hours in his day, and these hours should be used in a positive way to win souls and build his church.

40. *Talk about each success and forget about each failure.* A church planter will have to rejoice over small victories and count growth in small steps. A church moves forward from victory to victory, not by reliving the agonies of each defeat. The young pastor should promote the successes in the church to encourage new converts.

One church has posted a large sign consisting of three columns of statistics: (1) visitors sought, (2) visitors brought, and (3) new Christians. The first column suggests how many contacts were made, the second displays how many attended worship, and the third identifies those who made a decision for Christ or joined the church.

A new church should be victory-conscious, not obstacle-conscious. When God puts a vision in the heart of a church planter, it is for the "big view." Therefore, he must know where he is going and encourage his people every time they take a step toward that goal.

41. *Share the vision with the people.* Everything worthwhile is built on dreams, whether it is a marriage, a college education, or a new church. People will work, give sacrificially, and put up with temporary facilities if they have a dream from God of where they are going. To move the people, the church planter must share his vision/dreams with his people.

The church planter should try to instill an attitude of growth in his people. Anything other than expansion would be a traumatic experience to an infant congregation. So every time he challenges them to construct something new, they respond to leadership.

42. *Follow up with visitors.* Have a follow-up letter ready to send to all visitors who attend the first service. Also, attempt to get into the homes of visitors within a few days after they visit. The church planter's wife can phone during the day, especially if a family visited the new church. A woman-to-woman contact will not only be personal but effective.

43. *Establish an outreach program.* The question is often asked, "What type of outreach programs build a new church?" Some maintain that evangelism is the basis of building a church, and visitation should attempt to lead people to Christ. Others feel that a new church needs exposure. Therefore, the church planter should enlist as many helpers to contact as many people as possible, inviting them all to the new church.

The first is called an evangelistic contact, and the second is called friendship evangelism. Some great churches have been established by both methods, neither method excluding the other. By evangelistic visitation, new babes in Christ are brought into the church. This is the original purpose of all churches. However, house-to-house visitation will find mature Christians who may be languishing in dead churches. Those Christians can give money, teach classes, and win souls.

The visitation program will allow for the contacting of those people who have been made aware of your church as a result of advertising. Your church should have an active visitation program. Making friends is a vital part of visitation. Emphasize every visit primarily as a visit to present Jesus Christ and only secondarily as a church prospect call.

Should the church planter spend his time winning new converts or recruiting older Christians? When Carl Godwin was interviewing pastors before beginning his church in Nebraska, he asked about the foundation of a new church. Some pastors told Godwin not to proselytize older Christians from other churches because they had poor church habits and were usually the malcontents. "Go door-to-door and win your whole congregation to Christ," one pastor told Godwin, "then you have a church that will be pure and zealous to serve Christ." The older pastor continued, "These new Christians will follow your leadership and you can build a church without friction."

When Godwin founded Calvary Bible Church in Lincoln, he changed his thinking. His young Christians were not trained to come to Sunday services. They did not tithe, and some had problems with sins. These new babes in Christ were a thrill to Godwin, but they were not stable enough to help build a church. God sent to his church some mature Christians from other churches who could lead souls to Christ and teach Sunday school. These were not malcontents but were Christians who had been praying for an aggressive soul winning church in their city.

While Godwin was interviewing another pastor, he directed Godwin to get a nucleus of mature Christians to add stability to the young congregation. Some new churches are built almost exclusively on older Christians. These are people who have come out of another church, perhaps to preserve pure doctrine or to repudiate sin in the former assembly. These churches usually do not grow rapidly but do a commendable job of ministering the Word of God.

Sometimes old Christians have the stability of time-proven endurance, but they lack the zeal of the young convert who is carried along by his love for Christ.

Some church planters who have spent all their time telling people about Jesus at the front door of a home cannot get them to attend church. Sometimes they might want to establish relationships with people and get them to church. After people have heard the Gospel and received Christ, they are more likely to get involved in the church and grow in Christ.

The church planter faces the alternative of building his church on door-knocking (evangelism) or on ministering to mature Christians. The answer is neither extreme, but in a combination of the enthusiasm of young Christians and the maturity of the old. But, with this combination, never forget evangelism. The purpose of a church is winning the lost to Jesus Christ. Young churches, like the old ones, can lose their "first love" when they lose their soul winning perspective of evangelism.

44. Use authorities for credibility to the new church. I told Carl Godwin when he went to Lincoln that he should bring Christian authorities to speak to his people. These men would expand the vision of his people as well as substantiate his type of super-aggressive ministry. The people of Lincoln had never heard of a super-aggressive church that attempted to reach an entire city. They had always thought in terms of a local neighborhood parish church, the typical American view of Christianity.

Dr. Greg Dixon of Indianapolis Baptist Temple said that when his church was young and struggling, he had Dr. John Rawlings, pastor of one of the largest churches in America, come and preach for him. It gave young Dixon credibility in the eyes of the congregation, and it gave the young church credibility in the community's eyes. The church planter should attempt to schedule the following for his church:

▪ Pastors of large, recognized churches

▪ Educators of recognized colleges/seminaries

▪ Musicians

▪ Musical groups

45. *Find land for a permanent location.* Should a church planter choose a permanent location as soon as possible? It may not be possible to complete this step early in the life of a new church. Certain principles are important to remember. Some spend many hours looking for the correct location. It should to be (1) easily accessible, (2) centrally located, (3) not chosen because the ground was inexpensive or in an undesirable location, (4) large enough acreage, and (5) near a residential area where people are living. Pray over a map, and look at available property.

The permanent location of the church is highly important. Many young pastors have failed to realize the value of a good location. With the pressure of limited funds, they may settle for less expensive, out-of-the-way locations. The church planter should drive through the neighborhood and take note of (1) public schools; (2) shopping centers; (3) existing churches; (4) price and value of homes; (5) projection of new homes; (6) the size of building lots; (7) topography; (8) water, sewerage, and gas connections; (9) industrial and other barriers in the neighborhood; and (10) main arteries and thoroughfares.

The church planter should get the zoning ordinances in a city to determine restrictions on his proposed church. Some require a large paved parking lot with a low ratio of parking spaces to auditorium size, and others have no such restrictions. In a day of mobility, if zoning restrictions are severe, the pastor should look to the next municipality that is more conducive to building a church.

FOUR CRITERIA FOR A GOOD CHURCH SITE

1. Accessibility
2. Visibility
3. Relationship to the neighborhood
4. Adequacy

Accessibility. Accessibility means people have quick and easy access to the church site. Most of the members will travel by car, except for those who come by church bus. Very few will walk to the church. In our day of mobility, people will go as far to church as they drive to work. Some drive 40 miles one way to earn their paycheck. Hence, it is possible for a man to drive long distances to church. Studies have found that a man will drive 40 miles to church if it is located on the expressway. However, the same man would not drive five miles across the city in stop-and-go traffic, thinking that distance is too far. In metropolitan areas, people tend to judge distance by time rather than miles. Five minutes on the expressway is not as prohibitive as 15 minutes through traffic, even though it is half the distance.

Accessibility also means locating the church where the largest number of people are living. The people should have access to the church, and the church must also have access to the people.

Sometimes, the young church will have to buy property on the edge of the city before private homes are built. Hence, their members will have to drive out to the church. However, the church will be located in the middle of housing developments within five to ten years.

Whereas ten years ago, experts were counseling against locating a church on heavily traveled highways because of the danger to children, most church planters now maintain that a major artery is an excellent site. The danger to those who walk to Sunday school has disappeared. Of course, this principle applies to the United States, not other underdeveloped countries where many populations walk to church.

Visibility. The church should be visible to the neighborhood it desires to serve. If at all possible, place the building on a slight elevation so it can be seen from the street with the most traffic. Many churches have used signs to attract attention, but studies show that the public remembers the building better than any form of media.

Before purchasing the site, check the zoning to make sure that no tall buildings or industrial/commercial structures can be located next to the church. Not only would they hide the church from view, but the church's image could be lost among businesses. For some reason, Americans have a subconscious expectation that a church should be located in a residential neighborhood, not an industrial area.

One has even testified that a conspicuous site is worth more to a local church than a full-page advertisement in the newspaper every day of the year. This claim is probably exaggerated, but it does support the argument for a good location.

Relationship to the neighborhood plan. The church should be located near the focal point of the neighborhood. That way, residents pass it each day on their way to shop or work. If it is possible, locate the building near a shopping center so that the parking lot serves a dual purpose. Unfortunately, property near a shopping center is usually too expensive for a church.

A location near an elementary or high school is sometimes a focal point in the community. Here a church has accessibility and visibility. Also, it is near people, its point of ministry.

Adequacy. The church site must be adequate to complete its entire program. Whereas a few years ago, churches were buying four or five acres, now church planters are looking for ten acres or more. Some have even purchased a church campus of 100 acres. A building site may be attractive, but when considering a complete program, it may be far too small. If a church planter has a great vision, he will need a larger amount of space to carry out his ministry. Space is needed for parking, driveways, buildings, walkways, and expansion.

Check the master plan of the city to see if a future freeway or highway expansion will divide or partition part of your ground. Also, check other regulations such as setback requirements, floodplains, and amount of parking that will be allowed in the future. Some cities have not allowed churches to build on a large acreage because the property would be tax free. Some city fathers, feeling that they need tax income, will not zone a large acreage for a church campus.

If the site does not already have water, sewerage, and gas connections, the expense should be added to the total site cost. If a well must be dug or sewer lines constructed, the cost may be excessive. In some areas, a church may have to install septic tanks. For commercial use, they must be large and expensive. Some churches have had to build complete sewerage installation plants, costing over a million dollars.

A church planter should immediately begin looking for acreage. Owning property will give cohesiveness and permanence to a young congregation. As soon as new property is secured, place a sign that says, "Future Home of _____ Church." This will give the responsibility of ownership to your people and advertise your existence to the community.

46. *Don't build or buy a permanent facility too soon or too small.* At the same time, do not wait too long; some may leave a church if it is only renting facilities.

The acquisition of buildings and property is more important in American church growth than at other times in history. In the early church, Christians met on Solomon's porch for preaching and fellowship. Also, they met in private homes, in the school of Tyrannus, and in open amphitheaters and caves. There has always been some central focal place for assembly.

Since the second century of Christianity, Christians have constructed buildings. In our century, God has used many unusual locations to establish local churches. A boat house in Garland, Texas, launched the Lavon Drive Baptist Church. The Central Baptist Church in Phoenix, Arizona, first met around picnic tables in a park. Trinity Baptist Church in Chattanooga, Tennessee, was begun in a carport, and Calvary Baptist Church in Ft. Lauderdale, Florida, was begun in a display home. In addition to these, churches have been started in feed stores, fire departments, abandoned grocery stores, lodge halls, funeral homes, bankrupt soft drink bottling plants, and other buildings that brought a young congregation out of the elements.

As durable as these buildings were, an element of stability was added when a congregation moved into its own building.

Some advocate that a church should remain in rented facilities, not investing its money in buildings. One pastor desired to remain in a rented public school because the congregation was too poor to buy property and construct a building. To this day, they are still too poor and remain in the rented school. They argue that too much money is diverted from missions. As valid as this argument is, the church could have more in the future to give to missions by a stable location.

Church planters realize what moving into their own building can do to strengthen a young church. Rudy Holland in Roanoke, Virginia, indicated that many families remained on the fringe, watching the young church as it met in the rented facilities of the civic center. But when it moved into its own facilities, the attitude of Christians on the outside changed. Families began joining. These families brought financial strength, teaching abilities, and maturity with them.

When a congregation moves into its own facilities, it gains the following advantage: (1) the community realizes that the church is permanent, and no longer a transient group; (2) the young congregation becomes a part of the city, a property holder; (3) the young congregation identifies with the neighborhood, for they belong to the landscape and the community; and (4) permanent facilities allow people to funnel their energies into other ministries rather than preparing the building each week. One pastor indicated that each week he had to set up chairs, distribute hymnbooks, and get the building ready for a meeting.

When interviewing the pastors of the ten largest Sunday schools, most reiterated, "Never get out of a building campaign." By this they meant that a church should always plan another building for added growth. Christianity is a process, not a product. Therefore, the young congregation should always be building additional rooms or enlarging the auditorium. Physical expansion reflects spiritual growth, and if a church is winning souls, it will need more space to teach and preach. Also, when the neighborhood sees additions being built, they realize the church is growing.

Even though the building only houses the meetings of the church, Americans still judge a church by its buildings. Sloppily kept buildings indicate a messy attitude toward Christianity. When a congregation will sacrifice to build an auditorium, they tell the community that preaching is important.

ENDNOTES

CHAPTER 1

1. Elmer Towns, *Theology for Today* (Belmont, CA: Wadsworth/ Thompson Learning, 2002), 623-712. This is a systematic discussion of the church from a historical and doctoral perspective.

2. Elmer Towns, *Getting a Church Started: A Student Manual for the Theological Foundation and Practical Techniques of Planting a Church* (Lynchburg, VA: Church Growth Institute, 1985). *Planting Reproducing Churches* is the second book I have written on church planting. The first was a study of ten churches planted in the late 1960s and early 1970s.

3. Elmer Towns, ed., *A Practical Encyclopedia of Evangelism and Church Growth* (Ventura, CA: Regal Books, 1995), 251. This was the first book I wrote to explain the Great Commission was given five times. This book is more explanatory with references.

4. This formula based on arithmetic was first printed in Elmer Towns and Jerry Falwell, *Church Aflame* (Nashville, TN: Impact Books, 1971).

5. Jerry Falwell, *Capturing a Town for Christ* (Old Tappan, NJ: Fleming H. Revell, 1973), 84.

6. Statistics in this section received from Todd Wilson, www. startchurch.com.

7. Elmer Towns and Douglas Porter, *The Ten Greatest Revivals Ever*, 2nd ed. (Virginia Beach, VA: Academx Publishing Services, 2005), 214. Over the years, I have identified some evangelistic methods that appeared to be effective for a period of time, then lost their effectiveness. I've called these "anointed methods" to reflect those used by God, like people who are filled and anointed by the Holy Spirit. But both people and methods can lose their anointing.

8. "Cross-cultural Evangelism," in *A Practical Encyclopedia of Evangelism and Church Growth*, ed. Elmer Towns (Ventura, CA: Regal Books, 1995), 122.

9. Original research by Philip Jenkins, *The Next Christendom: The Rise of Global Christianity*, 3rd ed. (Oxford, UK: Oxford University Press, 2011).

10. "Martin Luther and the 95 Theses," *History.com*, accessed May 30, 2017, http://www.history.com/topics/martin-luther-and-the-95-theses.

11. Vinson Synan, "Chile's Super Church," in Towns, Vaughan, and Seifert, *The Complete Book of Church Growth*.

12. See http://en.wikipedia.org/wiki/Graha_Bethany_Nginden. Alex Tanuseputra founded the church in 1977. The church is affiliated with the International Church of God (Cleveland, Tennessee). He also has planted 700 churches on the various islands of Indonesia.

13. Information received from a conversation with Pastor Alex Tanuseputra while visiting Surabaya, Indonesia, in 2017.

14. See http://whcpageowner.wixsite.com/worldharvestcentre/about_us.

15. Suliasi Kurolo, *From the Ends of the Earth* (Indianapolis, IN: Christian Mission Fellowship International, 2014). See life story.

16. "The Unseen but Ever-Present Influence of House Churches," in Towns, *The Ten Most Influential Churches*, 39.

17. "Home Cells Used for Church Ministry and Outreach," in Towns, *The Ten Most Influential Churches*, 69-70.

18. Ibid., 70.

19. Towns, *The Ten Most Influential Churches*, 193.

20. Ibid., 193-94.

21. Ibid., 194.

22. Ibid.

CHAPTER 2

1. Elijah J.F. Kim, *The Rise of the Global South: The Decline of Western Christendom and the Rise of Majority World Christianity* (Eugene, OR: Wipf & Stock, 2012).

2. "Global Christianity: A Report on the Size and Distribution of the World's Christian Population," Pew Research Center, accessed May 23, 2017, http://www.pewforum.org/2011/12/19/global-christianity -exec/. Historical figures throughout the executive summary are courtesy of Todd M. Johnson of the Center for the Study of Global Christianity at Gordon-Conwell Theological Seminary in South Hamilton, Massachusetts. Johnson is coeditor of the *Atlas of Global Christianity* (Edinburgh University Press, 2009).

3. Ibid.

4. Philip Jenkins, *The Next Christendom: The Rise of Global Christianity* (Oxford, UK: Oxford University Press, 2011).

5. Ibid.

6. "Christianity in Africa," *Wikipedia*, accessed May 23, 2017, http:// en.wikipedia.org/wiki/Christianity_in_Africa.

7. Ibid.

8. "National Churches for Born-Again Churches," *UGO.CO.UG*, accessed May 23, 2017, http://directory.ugo.co.ug/listings/ national-fellowship-for-born-again-churches/.

9. Elmer Towns, "The World's Ten Largest Churches and How They Grew," *Christian Life Magazine*, January 1983, 60.

10. "Pentecostals & Charismatics in Latin America," Pew Research Center, accessed May 25, 2017, at http://www.pewforum. org/2006/10/05/overview-pentecostalism-in-latin-america/.

11. Ibid.

12. Ibid.

13. See Ed Silvoso, *Prayer Evangelism* (Ventura, CA: Regal Books, 2000) and *That None Should Perish* (Ada, MI: Chosen Books, 1995).

14. "Prayer Walk, Prayer Walking," *Dictionary of Christianese*, accessed May 25, 2017, http://www.dictionaryofchristianese.com/prayer-walk-prayer-walking/.

15. Hans Geir Aasmundsen, *Pentecostals, Politics, and Religion Equality in Argentina* (Leiden: Netherlands, 2016).

16 "Why Has Pentecostalism Grown So Dramatically in Latin America?" Pew Research Center, accessed May 25, 2017, http://www.pewresearch.org/fact-tank/2014/11/14/why-has-pentecostalism-grown-so-dramatically-in-latin-america/.

17. "International Pentecostal Holiness Church," *Wikipedia*, accessed May 25, 2017, at http://en.wikipedia.org/wiki/International_Pentecostal_Holiness_Church.

18. Alex Tanvsepata founded Bethany Church in 1977. Statement made in conversation with the author.

19. Kees de Jong, "The Growth of the Pentecostal-Charismatic Churches in Indonesia," *Exchange: Journal of Contemporary Christianity in Context*, 45 (2016): 195-201.

20. "Indonesia," *Wikipedia*, accessed May 25, 2017, http://en.wikipedia.org/wiki/Indonesia.

21. Tarheelhombre, *City-Data.com*, discussion board, posted on April 21, 2010, accessed May 25, 2017, http://www.city-data.com/forum/christianity/955925-christian-revolution-indonesia-fueled-megagrowth-pentecostals.html.

22. The usual definition of an indigenous church is that it is self-propagating, self-supporting, and self-governing. An indigenous church is completely self-reliant. The Communists recognized those churches because they had cut ties with foreign denominations and represented the Chinese culture.

23. Tom Phillips, "China on Course to Become 'World's Most Christian Nation' within 15 Years," *The Telegraph*, last modified April 19, 2014, http://www.telegraph.co.uk/news/worldnews/asia/china/10776023/

China-on-course-to-become-worlds-most-Christian-nation-within-15-years.html.

24. "The Top 20 Countries Where Christianity Is Growing the Fastest," *Disciple All Nations* (blog), last modified August 25, 2013, http://discipleallnations.wordpress.com/2013/08/25/THE-TOP-20-COUNTRIES-WHERE-CHRISTIANITY-IS-GROWING-THE-FASTEST/.

25. "Christianity in Korea," *Wikipedia*, accessed May 26, 2017, http://en.wikipedia.org/wiki/Christianity_in_Korea.

26. Ibid.

27. Ibid.

28. Warren Bird, "Korea: Why So Many Megachurches?" *Outreach Magazine*, last modified June 18, 2015, http://www.outreachmagazine.com/features/11955-why-so-many-megachurches-in-korea.html.

CHAPTER 3

1. Towns, *The Ten Most Influential Churches*, 76.

2. Ibid.

3. Ibid., 76-77.

4. Ibid.

5. Ibid., 77.

6. Towns, Vaughan, and Seifert, *The Complete Book of Church Growth*, 66.

7. "Cell Division," *Wikipedia*, accessed April 12, 2017, http://en.wikipedia.org/wiki/Cell_division.

8. Ibid.

9. "Apoptosis," *Wikipedia*, accessed May 19, 2017, http://en.wikipedia.org/wiki/Apoptosis.

10. James Egli and Dwight Marable, *Small Groups, Big Impact* (Saint Charles, IL: Churchsmart Resources, 2011).

11. Towns, Vaughan, and Seifert, *The Complete Book of Church Growth*, 62.

CHAPTER 4

1. Falwell, *Capturing a Town for Christ*, 84.

2. For a full discussion of the doctrine of blessability, see Towns, *God Bless You* (Ventura, CA: Regal Books, 2003). The glossary has 31 definitions of the various ways, persons, and results of blessings. The root meaning is "to add value." When God blesses a person's ministry, He adds His value to that ministry.

CHAPTER 5

1. However, capturing a town for Christ is a goal with limitations. What happens when the town is "captured" and a church is built? Every church should have a goal without limitations. What is a limitless goal? Planting reproducing churches that will plant other reproducing churches until the Great Commission is completed.

CHAPTER 8

1. Meeting with 22 house church leaders in Shanghai, China, October 19, 2009.
2. Neil Cole, *Organic Church* (San Francisco, CA: Jossey-Bass, 2005), xxii.

CHAPTER 9

1. Elmer Towns, "The Sociological Cycle of Church Life and Death," *America's Fastest Growing Churches* (Nashville, TN: Impact Books, 1972), 154.

CHAPTER 10

1. "Westminster Shorter Catechism," *Center for Reformed Theology and Apologetics*, accessed June 1, 2017, http://www.reformed.org/documents/wsc/index.html?_top=http://www.reformed.org/documents/WSC.html.
2 Robert Saucy, *The Church in God's Program* (Chicago, IL: Moody Press, 1972), 26.
3. Elmer Towns and Vernon Whaley, *Worship through the Ages* (Nashville, TN: B & H Academics, 2012), 2.
4. Saucy, *The Church in God's Program*, 33-34.
5. Ibid., 46.

6. Donald A. McGavran, *Understanding Church Growth* (Grand Rapids, MI: William B. Eerdmans, 1970), 4.

CHAPTER 11

1. Towns, *The Ten Largest Sunday Schools and What Makes Them Grow* (Grand Rapids, MI: Baker Book House, 1969).
2. This is a common "saying" that is used in Baptistic-type churches.
3. David R. Berman, *Politics, Labor and the War on Big Business* (Boulder, CO: University Press of Colorado, 2012), 117.
4. Vision statement of Saddleback Valley Community Church: "It is the dream of a place where the hurting, the depressed, the frustrated, and the confused can find love, acceptance, help, hope, forgiveness, guidance, and encouragement. It is the dream of sharing the Good News of Jesus Christ with the hundreds of thousands of residents in South Orange County. It is the dream of welcoming 20,000 members into the fellowship of our church family—loving, learning, laughing, and living in harmony together." Excerpted from the Society for Church Consulting's training, Aubrey Malphurs, instructor, accessed May 22, 2017, http://www.churchcentral.com/videos/analyzing-saddlebacks-vision-statement/.
5 A phrase often repeated by Jerry Falwell when instructing ministerial students to plant a church.
6. Towns, *Getting a Church Started*, 63-64.
7. Leon Morris, *Corinthians* (Grand Rapids, MI: William B. Eerdmans, 1958), 81.

CHAPTER 12

1. For sample lessons visit trbc.org/pbc.

FREE E-BOOKS?
YES, PLEASE!

Get **FREE** and deeply discounted **Christian books** for your **e-reader** delivered to your inbox **every week!**

IT'S SIMPLE!

VISIT lovetoreadclub.com

SUBSCRIBE by entering your email address

RECEIVE free and discounted e-book offers and inspiring articles delivered to your inbox every week!

Unsubscribe at any time.

SUBSCRIBE NOW!

LOVE TO READ CLUB

visit **LOVETOREADCLUB.COM** ▶

Made in the USA
Coppell, TX
10 December 2019